Options For The Teaching Of English

The Undergraduate Curriculum

Elizabeth Wooten Cowan
Series Editor

Published by The Modern Language Association of America
62 Fifth Avenue, New York, New York 10011

Contents

Introduction

"What is the shape of the undergraduate English curriculum in 1975?" asked a forme president of the Association of Departments of English at a recent committee meeting—casual question whose answer fills a book. This one. For no longer can we speak with at thority of *the curriculum*, as though that collective noun were shorthand for a set of ce tainties present in all departments. The varieties of curriculum organization and emphas represented by the accounts in this collection illustrate the assertion of departmen individuality. Some have changed; some haven't. Some want to; some don't. Some are e: cited; others, scared. Whatever their bent, the departments have provided, as in a stop motion frame, their programs, caught in time.

In spite of the diversity, certain generalizations about the undergraduate curriculum ca be drawn from the reports in this collection. Shakespeare appears on more lists of most pop ular courses than does any other English offering. British literature runs a far distant secon to American literature in student preferences, with British literature before 1900 the lea favored of all. Any course in modern literature is likely to be more popular than its counte parts from earlier times. Specialized period courses—for example, eighteenth-centur poetry, nineteenth-century prose—vie with survey courses for the designation of lea chosen courses in the curriculum. In fact, the eighteenth century is the period most ofte ignored by students, with Victorian and early English literature in close competition. Sing author, thematic, and topic courses are popular; both narrow and broad historical fram work courses are not. The juxtaposition of psychology with literature invariably brings st dents to a class; courses in fantasy, the quest for identity, myths and archetypes, for exan ple, are extremely popular on every campus where they are offered. While courses in fil and creative writing have very high enrollments in English departments all across the cou try, offerings in language and linguistics, in general, do not enjoy such popularity. Th teaching of advanced rhetorical writing to students in majors other than English increasing very rapidly; and freshman courses in writing appear to be receiving more atten tion than in the past. In fact, a trend seems to be emerging: the entire department is becom ing more and more involved in both freshman and advanced skills offerings. In more cas than not, students are allowed to put together their own majors, with minimal requiremen set by the department; and comprehensive examinations are quite rare. While the number majors continues to hold steady at best, if not to decline, most departments represented he are teaching as many or more students than in years before; basic skills courses and exper mental and innovative offerings probably account for this.

Objective reportage is the aim of this book. No value judgments are made or intende Colleges and universities were invited to contribute according to geography, size, camp setting, and type of school. Some accepted the invitation but were unable to meet the dea line. Others declined the invitation too late to be replaced. Representation, however, h. been achieved from every section of the country, from every four-year category set up b the Carnegie Commission on Higher Education in *A Classification of Institutions of High Education*, and from small/large, urban/rural colleges and universities.

Options for the Teaching of English: The Undergraduate Curriculum is the first book i a series, sponsored by the Modern Language Association and its Committee on Pedagogic. Publications and endorsed by the Association of Departments of English, which is designe to cover in depth in separate volumes specific aspects of the college English curriculun Future topics will include the teaching of freshman English, interdisciplinary courses an programs, and college/university teaching of advanced writing.

Elizabeth Wooten Cowan
Director, English Program, ML.
Coordinator, ADE

iv

1

3all State University

)ur regular faculty are now teaching more general studies courses on the freshman level.

:hairman Dick Renner
Ball State University
Muncie, Indiana 47306

'ull-Time Faculty 47½

:alendar Quarter

Fype of School Public doctoral-granting university

Requirements for Major Teaching Major, 60 quarter hours; Departmental Major, ▪0 or 48 quarter hours, depending upon program. English Qualifying Test taken at ▪eginning of sophomore year.

The undergraduate English curriculum at Ball State University is the product of the opportunities, dilemmas, and challenges confronting this recently emerged state university in Indiana. The opportunities began when enrollments increased by nearly 1,000 students per year during the decade of the 1960's; the dilemmas and challenges developed when decreasing enrollments, the shifting job market, and nearly open admission policies in the early 1970's resulted in significant annual declines in English majors and minors but steady annual increases in freshmen admitted on "warning status."

National population growth, the Viet Nam war, a national shortage of English teachers, Indiana's new certification requirement of a completed master's degree within five years of graduation with a bachelor's degree in a teaching area, and Ball State's national record of excellence in teacher training probably were the primary causes of the tremendous increase in Ball State's enrollments during the 1960's. The English department responded quickly to the opportunity to educate these increased numbers of students, many of whom were the first in their families ever to attend a university. It designed special general studies courses for academically talented freshmen, revised existing courses, and added new courses in American literature, British literature, language and linguistics, and English education. It also enlarged its faculty in order to meet the educational needs and interests of the increasing number of students pursuing English majors or minors on either the bachelor's or the master's level.

The shifting job market for teachers during the past five years and the declining enrollments during the past two years, however, have presented serious problems. With an annual decline of approximately five percent in total undergraduate enrollments and approximately thirty percent in undergraduate English teaching majors and minors, the English department has been confronted with several dilemmas. With a highly qualified, specialized regular faculty to support its seven undergraduate and five graduate programs but with declines in the number of its majors and minors on the bachelors and masters levels, the department has been obliged to compensate by assigning its regular faculty to teach a larger portion of the general studies courses in English. Consequently, annual reductions have been necessary in the number of temporary positions available for part-time and full-time instructors, most of whom either were pursuing doctoral studies or recently had completed masters studies. Inflationary costs of nonpersonnel expenses, reduced revenues from reduced enrollments, and the subsequent reduction of monies available for faculty positions have increased the teaching loads of the regular faculty and decreased the time available for individual research and writing.

At the same time, a new challenge has confronted the department as the result of the university's shift to a nearly open admission policy. The SAT scores and high school ranks of students admitted on "warning status" indicated that additional special courses and tutorial assistance would be needed if these probationary students were to have successful educational experiences. The department accepted the challenge and attempted to meet these special needs in special sections of the required general studies courses; but success was minimal. Consequently, following in part a successful model already established for international students, the department added a pre-general studies course in the fundamentals of English grammar and provided free supplementary tutoring in the department's Writing Clinic. The results have been highly satisfactory—in fact, much better than anticipated.

Within this historical framework, the present undergraduate English curriculum of more than sixty courses—each offered at least once each academic year and once each summer—is designed to meet the academic needs and interests of six groups of students: (1) international students and "warning-status" freshmen needing pre-general studies instruction in the fundamentals of English grammar and usage; (2) general university students needing instruction in freshman writing and reading skills, as required by the University General Studies Program; (3) academically talented students planning to participate in the University Honors Program; (4) English and elementary education majors and minors studying for careers in teaching; (5) English majors and minors planning either to continue graduate studies in English or to pursue nonteaching careers; and (6) students with majors and minors in areas outside English who wish to supplement their studies with English courses.

The English courses designed to meet the special needs of the international students and the "warning-status" freshmen stress the fundamental skills of English grammar and usage. Demonstrated proficiency in these skills usually enables these students to continue successfully in the general studies sequence of English courses as required in the University General Studies Program.

English courses in the general studies sequence are rather traditional and consist of (1) a course of freshman composition, including a functional review of major distinctions in grammar and usage and the study of expository prose, considered a practical necessity for most university students; (2) a second course in freshman composition, including the study of poetry and drama and the writing of a research paper, considered necessary as preparation for writing and research required in subsequent university studies; and (3) a sophomore course in world literature, primarily prose fiction, for students not planning to major or minor in the humanities. Majors or minors in an area of the humanities—including English—are exempt from this third general studies course.

Special sections of the second freshman composition course, a sequence of three sophomore honors humanities courses, an honors colloquium, and an interdepartmental senior honors project are offered by the English department for academically talented students participating in the University Honors Program. These courses and colloquia are designed to introduce some of the major myths, philosophies, and literary works of Western civilization and to direct independent research on selected issues in English.

The courses designed for students pursuing any of the seven undergraduate major or minor programs in English consist primarily of traditional survey and advanced courses in world, American, and British literature; basic courses in the study of the history and structure of the English language; advanced courses in creative, expository, and critical writing; and those methodology courses required for secondary English and elementary education teachers. Advanced period courses are available in world, American, and British poetry, drama, and fiction; seminars cover the works of individual writers. In addition, advanced courses are offered in specialized areas of interest, such as folklore, Black literature, and adolescent literature. All of these courses include a careful study of the primary subject matter; many also include library research for class reports and research papers. All are open to non-English majors and minors wishing to supplement their studies.

Many of the general studies English courses are taught by graduate assistants, doctoral fellows, part-time and full-time instructors (all of whom are pursuing graduate English programs); however, 50 percent of these courses are taught by the 48 regular faculty members in the department. All other English courses are taught only by the regular faculty, of whom 46 have doctorates.

Because of the university's increasing emphasis on scholarly research and publications by the faculty, the regular faculty in the English department have found it difficult to reduce their smorgasbord of advanced undergraduate courses, even though the number of undergraduate English majors and minors continues to decline significantly each year. Having expanded their undergraduate and graduate course offerings to meet the needs of the 1960's and the challenges of the 1970's, the faculty are reluctant to drop undergraduate courses in their respective areas of expertise. The solution thus far has been to retain the numerous undergraduate courses in specialized areas and, if necessary, with appropriate adjustments in course requirements, teach them together with similar graduate courses and seminars. Herein, however, probably lies an important weakness in the department's undergraduate curriculum.

The department has not in recent years implemented either extensive or radical changes in its undergraduate curriculum, but those implemented have been rather significant. For example, several courses designed for non-English majors and minors were dropped during the teacher education boom of the 1960's, but recently these same courses have been resurrected to meet the current interests of students with majors and minors in fields other than English. The earlier, special track of general studies courses for the academically talented has been replaced with an option of credit by examination (e.g., SAT, CEEB, or departmental), and special courses have been added for international students and "warning-status" freshmen. All undergraduate English courses, moreover, with the exception of four, have been changed to four quarter hours each, thus reducing the number of English courses required.

Special courses and sections also have been added for students participating in the quarter programs at Ball State University's London Centre and Chicago Urban Field Study Project; those participating in the University Honors Program, the Residential Instruction Project, and the local experimental program in elementary education (EXEL); those interested in specialized courses such as folklore, Black literature, adolescent literature, and women in literature; and those pursuing major or minor programs in other departments but wishing to supplement their studies with English courses.

In addition, some courses (particularly those in general studies) have been modified somewhat to meet the unique academic needs and interests of students attending classes at Grissom Air Force Base or other off-campus locations in the eastern half of Indiana. Plans also are in process to design new off-campus courses to meet the needs and interests of other specific professional or age groups.

In spite of these efforts, the department has not been able to halt the steady decline of English majors and minors. The problems caused by the present oversupply of English teachers and the limited funds to employ additional qualified teachers in the public schools, however, cannot be solved by the English department or the university. Neither can the English faculty obliterate most students' natural fears of freshman composition and some English majors' and minors' apprehensions of reputedly difficult courses such as advanced composition, historical development of the English language, and modern English grammar. Similarly, the English faculty cannot necessarily change the preferences of certain students for courses that seem to them to be more familiar and relevant; for example, courses in modern American literature. On the other hand, the teaching excellence of many English professors can and does motivate students to take advanced courses in less familiar, though often more traditional, areas of English study.

Moreover, the English department at Ball State University is committed to an ongoing coordination, evaluation, and improvement of its undergraduate curriculum to meet its present and future opportunities, dilemmas, and challenges. Its English Undergraduate Programs Committee, established in the spring of 1973, already has helped to mobilize the total resources of the department toward these goals. This mobilization has resulted, for example, in the initiation of new procedures for the recruitment of English majors and minors; the development of new courses and programs in English and in conjunction with academic programs in other areas; and the establishment of a subcommittee of department mentors to assist undergraduate English majors and minors in program planning, course selection, and job placement. Other ideas and procedures from faculty, students, and graduates will, of course, continue to be given careful consideration by the entire department in the hope that the undergraduate English curriculum at Ball State University will meet the academic needs and interests of its present and future students.

Daryl B. Adrian
Associate Professor of English

Typical Courses Added in the Last Five Years
Fundamentals of English Composition
Technical Report Writing
Literature of Black America
Honors Colloquium in English
Literature for Adolescents
Advanced Expository Writing and Literature
Special Topics in World, American, and British Literature
Independent Study in Literature
American Literature, 1945 to Present
Studies in English Literature of the Age of Johnson
Myth and Identity
Modern British Poetry

Typical Courses Dropped in the Last Five Years
Literature and Composition for Foreign Students
Twentieth-Century British Studies

High Enrollment Courses
Modern American Literature
Language and Linguistics
Children's Literature

Shakespeare
Drama

Decreased Enrollment Courses
Advanced Composition
The English Language
English Literature of the Middle Ages and Renaissance
The Teaching of Language Arts in the Upper Elementary Grades
English Drama from Medieval Times to 1642
Literature of Black America
American Folklore

Courses Drawing Nonmajors
Literature of Black America
Technical Report Writing*
Advanced Expository Writing and Literature*
Short Story*
The Essay*
Special Topics in World, American, and British Literature*

Courses Most Attractive to Majors
American and British Literature

Designed specifically to meet the interests and needs of nonmajors.

Major Changes in Curriculum
(1) All advanced courses have been changed from three to four hours, thus reducing the number of courses required for a major; (2) the twelve-hour requirement of Latin 217, Philosophy 100, and History 475 or 476 for all departmental majors has been changed from required to recommended; (3) advanced courses and their graduate counterpart are taught together; (4) more advanced courses are offered on campus during evenings and at off-campus locations; (5) an English department mentor system has been established to assist students in academic program planning, course selections, and job placement.

2

Carleton College

Advanced Rhetoric, after limping along for years, by 1974 had become the largest course on campus, with the exception of spring baseball.

Chairman Harriet Sheridan
Carleton College
Northfield, Minnesota 55057

Full-Time Faculty 15

Calendar Trimester

Type of School Private liberal arts

Requirements for Major Sixty credits including English Literature, one course within five of the following eight areas: (1) Chaucer, Medieval and Renaissance Literature, Spenser; (2) Shakespeare; (3) Seventeenth Century, Milton; (4) Eighteenth Century; (5) American Literature; (6) Romantics, Victorian Literature, Nineteenth-Century Fiction; (7) Twentieth Century; (8) History of English Language, Linguistics. Senior seminar, twelve credits in literature other than English read either in the original language or in translation (Greek and Latin particularly recommended), comprehensive examination based on departmental reading list.

Most people would remark that the two most evident of the recent changes in the quality of life at Carleton—the near doubling of the enrollment and the shifting of the calendar from the semester to the three-term system—have had the greatest effect on the manner in which the English department operates. The roughest kind of head-counting, with no attention paid to full-time equivalents and other niceties that deans and computers affect, shows that during the past eight or nine years the department has grown and become busier: about nine years ago 11 teachers made 40 full-scale classroom performances per year; now 17 teachers make 55. Besides, the popularity of Independent Study and the necessity that it be supervised can add as many as six extra courses to the work of those teachers eager or foolish enough to undertake the guiding of the allowed maximum of two independent studiers per term. The independent studier is obviously always interested in something that no one on the staff happens to be teaching.

Teachers who have been here during this time of change will agree that the worst difficulty the increase in student population has caused is in the managing of the course we have at various times called Freshman English, Rhetoric, and Writing Seminar. Because we have tried to limit the sections in Rhetoric to fifteen students each, the number of sections increased with the number of students. One solution was to cut back on the requirement: where once students were given fifteen weeks of Rhetoric plus another fifteen if they needed it, they are now expected to get enough training in ten weeks (though more time is made available to those who need it). Another solution was to exempt certain students from the requirement in Rhetoric: a committee of the department would read the writings of students who thought they deserved exemption and then make decisions most of the members considered rational. Neither of these solutions is perfect, but the department struggles along with them, each teacher meeting his Rhetoric sections two or three times a week, and during the ten-week course holding four or more individual conferences with each student during which the writing of the student is analyzed and criticized. Some teachers also are responsible for the teaching of special sections established to match the diversity in ability that accompanies the increase in numbers of students.

In recent years the description of Rhetoric as "a course in reading and writing required of all freshmen" disappeared from the catalog and was replaced by something called "the college writing proficiency requirement." The reasons for this are politically obscure and educationally complicated, but a fancier of noun adjuncts can make an analysis of the new description and a guess as to whence it might have emanated. Still, although the new definition has raised questions in some minds about the difference between having to pass a certain course and having to attain a proficiency, it has for the first time here pointed to a formal recognition of the fact that teachers in departments other than English may assume the responsibility of judging a student's ability to read and write well. This past summer students and teachers from various departments met in a two-week conference at which they discussed, and came to some kind of consensus about, how one may first inspire or produce and then recognize a "college writing proficiency." And the 1974-75 academic year is the first during which students may prove their ability as writers by writing not solely as producers of "freshman themes" but as students of literature, philosophy, history, and classical languages. It bodes well for the success of this venture that all those who took part in the institute were volunteers. Members of the department believe that what we still think of as Rhetoric is the most important part of our curriculum, and it has long been the custom that all members, from the most junior up to and including the most senior, have a part in the teaching of it. We are, however, not agreed on what are the best textbooks or the best methods to use. Our various chairmen have for many years recognized this and have permitted each teacher to select texts to his liking and to use procedures in which he is comfortable. One attempt to require all teachers to use the same "handbook" in order that some uniformity in punctuation might result came close to being a failure; some teachers thought the handbook was too prescriptive and others thought it was silly. And in one term one teacher decided to teach the course without using any text at all. He had a pretty good time, and some of the students said that they did too.

Our curriculum in toto is the result of this way of thinking. Although the "most evident of the recent changes" have of course affected the department's manner of operation, the dominant forces shaping the curriculum itself have not been the pressure of an increased population or the change in calendar. During the last decade, the important and effective influences on the curriculum have been the students as students and not as population, and the teachers as teachers and not as academic theoreticians. It might not be wrong to say that in making decisions concerning the curriculum the department has been run or has run itself much in the manner of a Quaker meeting. In fact, strangers who have been present at departmental meetings have frequently remarked on the quietness with which matters are decided.

This reflects the quietness with which new members of the department are selected. A candidate for a position will give a lecture open to students and faculty of all departments, attend a few receptions and parties, and after two or three days go his way. The chairman, in a series of private conversations, then discovers what is the prevailing feeling, and the final decision is made in the upper echelons. In this way we have added to our ranks some people with political ambition, some with revolutionary instincts, and even some with an abiding love of literature. But only rarely have we added a new member unable to cope with the quiet stubbornness with which decisions regarding our curriculum are made in departmental meetings.

At these meetings all hands are permitted to make proposals concerning the curriculum. The young instructor might want to teach his dissertation even before it is typed. The elder professor, who, under the weight of his long experience, has suddenly found exactly the proper load he would like all schoolboys and colleagues to carry, might want to legislate universal erudition. The proposals are argued, sometimes dropped simply because only the sponsor is interested, sometimes allowed to sink because of the sheer bulk of the paper involved in three extensive revisions. Sometimes, of course, the proposal is adopted. And sometimes the decision is to "type it up and circulate it among the majors and see what happens." One recent and very elaborate proposal died because fewer students than teachers were interested in it. In contrast, a course in Advanced Rhetoric and Composition, taught by a team of three teachers, was revived at the request of students increasingly aware of their weaknesses as writers. It has been heavily subscribed.

A curriculum formed in this way is naturally the result of a series of compromises. And our "Requirements for a Major" can be read as a compromise between those students and teachers who would like the major to be a series of courses carefully engineered and arranged to cover the works of the major writers and to explain the chronological development of our literature and, on the other hand, those who would prefer that the major permit the greatest possible freedom of inquiry and individual inventiveness. We offer three introductory survey courses: the first covering Chaucer to Milton and the seventeenth-century lyric poets, the second covering the neoclassic to the Victorian, and the third being an introduction to modern literature. We credit only the first two toward the major, hoping thus to force at least a cursory look at the chronological relations and even requiring that these two introductions be taken before the student is admitted to upperclass courses. So much for the hard-nosed approach. Against it the libertarians have arranged that upperclass courses be divided into eight groups (e.g., the Chaucer, Studies in the Renaissance, Spenser group) and have required for the major a satisfactory performance in one course from each of five of these groups. This arrangement makes it possible for the student to complete his major without having had any guided or supervised reading in Shakespeare other than that he gets in his exposure to several plays in the introductory survey, although this is unlikely to be the case. It also allows him to have credit for a number of courses with ambiguous titles and doubtful relationships that may or may not lead him to decide whether he has been dealing with one or three subjects. Upon the free-form finger painting that this arrangement makes possible, the traditionalists have been able to impose a focus and discipline by distributing to the majors a departmental reading list that they will be examined on before they can be certified as having met the requirements for a major.

Members of the department are satisfied with this system. Despite the occasional revolutionary proposal, the present system has survived with few changes in the past four or five years. The fact is that no significant or influential groups of students have seceded and no teachers have attempted to establish a Rump Department. And another fact is that we have not been able to determine what courses or what tracks are more popular than others. The same course will have a large enrollment one year and a smaller one the next. But at least one member of the department thinks he has detected a trend. He was overheard to say that this year many more "good students" are making calls in the office of our most aloof disciplinarian-traditionalist than in recent years have been beating a path to the office of our "bleeding heart," our "natural man." Trends, obviously, are where you find them if you stay around long enough for the turn of the wheel.

Erling Larsen
Emeritus Professor of English

Typical Courses Added in the Last Five Years
The Theatre in Society
Writing Colloquium
Introduction to Literary Study
Introduction to Film
Studies in Renaissance Literature
Nineteenth-Century Fiction
Writing Tutorial
The Bible in English Literature
Poetry, Magic, and Nonsense
Controversy: The Art of Spoken Argument
Rhetoric-Composition
The Crafts of Writing
Seminar: Directing
Special Problems in Writing and Reading

Special Authors
Special Topics

Typical Courses Dropped in the Last Five Years
English Literature, 1830-1870
English Literature, 1870-1914
Practical Criticism
Survey of Medieval Literature
Special Problems in Writing and Reading
The Bible in English Literature
Special Authors

Most Popular Courses
Contemporary Fiction

Novel
Shakespeare
American Literature
Advanced Rhetoric

American Literature
Film
Linguistics and History of the English
  Language

Least Popular Courses
Upper division specialized courses

Courses Most Attractive to Nonmajors
Introductory level literature courses
Advanced Rhetoric

Courses Most Attractive to Majors
American Literature
Advanced Rhetoric
Shakespeare
Author and period courses rather than theme
  or genre

Major Changes in Curriculum
(1) For majors, the requirement of twelve credits in history and eight in philosophy has been dropped; the requirement of one upperclass foreign language was replaced by the alternative of two courses in a literature other than English; and a senior seminar has been added as a requirement; (2) alternatives for fulfilling the college writing requirement now allow students to work for a satisfactory rating in one of three kinds of courses: (a) English 1, Writing Seminar, (b) English 10, 11, 12, (c) introductory level courses in Greek 34, Art 11, Arts and Sciences 20, History 12, Section 1, History 12, Section 4 (category c courses are underlined in the schedule). In courses in categories b and c, the usual credit arrangements will prevail, but two grades will be given: the grade for the course, and for those students who have shown a satisfactory level of writing skill, an *S* for writing. A student who does not receive an *S* is advised to take English 1 in the succeeding term, but may try again in the two latter categories. The *S* rating will be reported to the student by the English department. Registration of those who want to fulfill the writing requirement as well as take the course in categories b and c is limited to ten students per course. They will receive a special registration card in addition to the regular course card. English 1, Writing Seminar, devotes itself intensely to the improvement of writing skill by requiring a minimum of ten themes and revisions; some sections emphasize the command of spoken language as well. Courses in the other two categories require fewer essays, but will ask for revisions. Similar standards for evaluation apply to all three kinds of courses. A student who does not come up to competency must continue on in writing courses until his or her skill has reached a satisfactory state. Exemption from the college writing requirement is given to entering freshmen *solely* on the basis of scores on the CEEB Advanced Placement Examination in Composition (taken at the conclusion of a high school Advanced Placement in Composition course); it is *never* given on the basis of SAT verbal scores.

3

Carnegie-Mellon University

The writing options are the most rapidly growing areas of the English department at Carnegie-Mellon.

Chairman Arthur Eastman
Carnegie-Mellon University
Schenley Park
Pittsburgh, Pennsylvania 15213

Full-Time Faculty 27

Calendar Semester

Type of School Private research university

Requirements for Major Regular Major: 93-105 units (31-35 credits), Shakespeare one genre course, two period courses, two author courses, three English elective courses. No comprehensive examination. Requirements vary in other options.

The heterogeneous nature of Carnegie-Mellon serves to explain something of the nature of the English major, and a bit of history will perhaps provide helpful background. The English department was a service unit for the entire school from the founding of Carnegie Institute of Technology early in this century until the creation of the College of Humanities and Social Sciences in 1969. However, during that time and within the framework of the Margaret Morrison Carnegie College for Women, it was possible for women to major in English. This regularly happened at the rate of some ten to twelve graduates a year.

With the founding of the liberal arts college in 1969, the departments of English, history, psychology, and modern languages began to attract men and women in almost equal numbers. There were approximately 200 English majors in 1969. Today, in a college of some 700 (the total undergraduate enrollment at Carnegie is kept at about 3,000) there are about 250 English majors, with approximately 50 graduates each year.

These graduates are divided in roughly the following way: the regular English option, with major focus on courses in literature; the writing option, divided into creative, critical, or technical writing and editing; and the teacher training option, a small but steady group of majors headed for high school or elementary teaching. About a third of the graduates fall under the traditional English literature option; about a third comprise the various writing programs, the creative and critical principally; the remainder are divided among the Bachelor of Science in Technical Writing and Editing, the teacher training program, and those students working for a double major, the second major falling normally to history, psychology, or modern languages.

Thus, the traditional B.A. in English found in many small liberal arts colleges is much less prominent at Carnegie. Few of its graduates choose to go on to graduate school in English, though this is perhaps not unique at Carnegie in these days of economic stress. Rather, the professional emphasis within the English major is prominent and increasing. This is not surprising in a university with the oldest, and one of the best, undergraduate drama schools in the nation, and with engineering and science colleges that rank with the best in the country. Economic conditions, too, have led many English majors to want a professional, "useful" component in their degrees.

For the regular English major there are nine required courses in English beyond The Literary Imagination, which is the freshman English course: Shakespeare, two period courses, two author seminars, one genre course, and three elective English courses. The period courses and author seminars, for juniors and seniors, are designed to be challenging. For creative (fiction, poetry) and critical writing majors we require Shakespeare, one period course, one author seminar, and one elective course. But the core of the creative writing major begins with a two-semester introductory course called Survey of Genres. The writing student then goes on to pursue either poetry or fiction in four writing workshops, small (20-student maximum) informal classes in which students criticize their own work under the guidance of a publishing writer of poetry or fiction. The critical or free-lance writers also pursue a series of writing courses and workshops, and some few combine these with courses in playwriting offered by the drama department.

For the technical writing and editing majors there is also a sequence of writing courses: Exposition I and II, in which the student works at perfecting clarity of style and awareness of audience; Exposition III, in which he is introduced to the actual variety and skills of writing for business or industry, again, by a practicing professional writer; and Exposition IV, which consists of 100 hours of on-the-job internship with local business or industry. This series of writing courses for the technical writers combines with courses in mathematics, physics, chemistry, biology, and other physical and social sciences to give the technical writing major a wide experience in areas of potential employment. The students take two courses in graphic design fundamentals to add to their range of experience. Study of computer science and statistics is on the upswing with this option.

The teaching option consists primarily of a Professional Semester, offered in the fall semester of the senior year. Within it the student has courses in methods and two distinct experiences of practice teaching in the local high schools. This teaching is closely supervised both by a critic-teacher in the school and by a trained member of the English department staff. In addition, there are required courses in advanced writing, oral communication, and cognitive processes. The small number (about 10 students a year) allows for learning experience in considerable depth.

Training for elementary school teaching is a cooperative venture with Chatham College. The actual educational courses and practice teaching are supervised by Chatham personnel, and the practice teaching extends across the senior year.

At the moment, the writing options are the most rapidly growing areas of the English department at Carnegie-Mellon. The training in each area is rigorous and thoroughly professional, and the job market has responded well to these degree-holders.

Of course, the English department offerings (some 50 courses each semester, including a number of sections of The Literary Imagination) serve the entire university as well as the English majors. In general, the department is popular within the university. Its teachers receive high ratings in schoolwide student evaluations, and the elective offerings are often forced to turn prospective students away.

Three areas seem currently of greatest interest to students, both English and non-English majors: offerings in modern literature, Shakespeare, and film courses. The department currently offers a series of three film courses—Film Art, History of Film Styles, and Film and Literature—and hopes to add a fourth course in Script Writing to the series soon. Shakespeare, perhaps because the English faculty contains many members who are expert or enthusiastic in the area, draws widely from across the campus.

Again, probably because of the heterogeneity of the Carnegie undergraduate population, courses in modern literature draw amazing numbers of students. A current course in the Literature of the American Twenties and Thirties has over 100 students in two sections. The course in Film Art drew well over 100 last spring. And the department offers three sections of Shakespeare each semester, each with a maximum of 45 students, and each normally filled to that limit.

The author seminars, held to fifteen students each, are always filled, but most rapidly when their subjects are modern writers like Faulkner, Kafka, Lawrence, Mann, Camus, and Dostoyevsky. Students definitely wish to know about modern writers other than those from England and America. They prefer to study in depth rather than widely, and the department does not offer survey courses of any kind except on rare occasions.

Courses like Modern or Contemporary Novel, Continental Drama, and Biblical and Mythological Backgrounds of English Literature are popular with nonmajors, along with such thematic courses as The Quest for Identity, Rites of Passage, and Mystic and Visionary Poets. Such a course as Literature and the Other Arts draws a cross-section of students, as does a course in Imaginative Literature of the Far East.

The courses least popular these days are those that focus on eighteenth-century English literature. The Age of Reason seems to turn students away, while the areas of literature that are "Romantic" seem to attract them. The traditional focus, then, on English and American literature is rapidly giving way to a much broader spectrum of course offerings. Students are curious about the literatures of Europe and the Third World and are increasingly impatient with the chronological study of literature.

There has been an upsurge in demand for expository writing courses from all parts of the campus, and it seems that students are truly beginning to realize that this skill is a valuable one, both in undergraduate study and for the future. But this poses a considerable challenge to the English faculty, many of whom are having to work very hard to find viable ways to teach exposition.

A final note: Carnegie-Mellon's English department continues to attract students primarily because of the personalized education it offers. Classes are small, with twenty-five as an average. Students and teachers get to know each other both for this reason and because of the close adviser-student relationships. English majors serve on all departmental committees and have a genuine input in department affairs, as to both course offerings and the changing shape of the major requirements in all English major options.

Beekman W. Cottrell
Director, Undergraduate Studies in English

Typical Courses Added in the Last Five Years
Biblical and Mythological Backgrounds
    of English Literature
The Quest for Identity
Plato and the Concept of Love
Medieval Epic and Prose before 1300
Women in the Literature of Victorian
    England: Repression and Revolt
Black and White in American Literature
Rites of Passage
The Writer in the Colonized Society
Shakespeare's Complete Works, I and II
Freud (and Marx, separately) in Twentieth-
    Century Literary Criticism
Film Art
The History of Film Styles
Mystics and Visionary Poets

Typical Courses Dropped in the Last Five Years
Applied Public Speaking
The Nature and Function of Language
Science Fiction
Modern Writers
Survey of English Literature I and II

Most Popular Courses
Film
Courses in modern literature
Writing workshops
Free-Lance Writing
The New Journalism
Seminar courses in such European writers as
    Mann, Camus, Kazantzakis
Thematic courses such as Rites of Passage
    and The Quest for Identity

Least Popular Courses
Courses falling into narrow historical
    framework
Survey courses
Eighteenth-century literature

Courses Most Attractive to Nonmajors
Film
Modern literature
Writing workshops
European or Far Eastern literature

Courses Most Attractive to Majors
Many of the above but also author seminars
    that study writers in depth—Joyce,
    Faulkner, the Greek playwrights

4

University of Chicago

We could fill courses in modern fantasy, modern novel, film, and so on many times over.

Chairman Stuart M. Tave
University of Chicago
1050 East 59th Street
Chicago, Illinois 60637

Full-Time Faculty 34

Calendar Quarter

Type of School Private research university

Requirements for Major Twelve quarter-long courses, each three hours credit. During senior year, English major selects one of four programs: reading tutorial, independent research, seminar, or elective.

To describe the undergraduate concentration in English language and literature at the University of Chicago in the academic year 1974-75 is to catch what is probably the most unrepresentative moment in the history of a curriculum that has been characterized by increasingly rapid changes. A series of committee reports, recommending improvements or total reform of then current programs, testify to the indefatigable pursuit of the perfect curriculum by generation after generation of faculty and students. Before the mid sixties though, before student unrest widened to include both political and academic dissatisfaction, the curriculum was reformed at a relatively leisurely pace, with one major change every eight years or so. Since the mid sixties, the pace has quickened, each change speaking more quickly to the perceived shortcomings of the previous program and to the new realities of higher education. To understand where we are and where we may be going, then, requires historical as well as pedagogical understanding.

The stated aims of those programs in the fifties and sixties were to develop in the student the ability to criticize imaginative texts, to analyze intellectual prose, and to know literary history. To achieve these objectives, the English department required of its majors twelve courses. Six were specified: one course in poetry, one in intellectual prose or literary criticism, two courses in English and one in American literary history, and one course in Shakespeare. All programs also had to include at least one course from a period earlier than 1660, one in literature written between 1600 and 1800, and one in literature between 1800 and 1900. Genre courses could satisfy historical distribution requirements. In addition, English majors were expected to take as an outside elective a three-quarter course on English history.

At the end of the junior year, students took a three-hour qualifying examination on a set list of texts, an examination that stressed factual knowledge of literature. At the end of the senior year, majors had to pass the B.A. final, a six-hour exam based on a shorter list of works that stressed critical analysis and writing ability. To provide time for the independent reading required for the junior qualifying exam, students registered for a three-quarter sequence of reading courses. They prepared for the final on their own.

This program was the result of an even earlier one, when the college had no "major" as we know it now, but only a general education program lasting about four years for those students entering after the tenth grade, three years for those entering after the eleventh grade. In 1954, when the undergraduate program was revised, part of a very demanding three-year M.A. program, examinations and all, was simply grafted onto the undergraduate program as a B.A. concentration.

In 1966 the program was revised. The junior examination was dropped. The course requirements were changed to stipulate one course each in literary criticism, literary historiography, and Shakespeare, two courses stressing the relationship of English literature to its historical or intellectual context, and one of the same sort in American literature. No period distribution was required. Six other electives would also be chosen by the student after consultation with his faculty adviser.

These programs all built on the strengths of what has come to be known as the Chicago School of Criticism: an interest in formulating questions appropriate to a text in terms of its intrinsic nature and in understanding the assumptions behind those questions. The interest was supported by the college-wide requirements that expected every undergraduate to pursue three yearlong sequences in the humanities. But if the program trained the students to be sophisticated critics, it was said that it slighted their control of historical facts and contexts and often failed to expose students to some of the major texts, a suspicion reflected in the fact that many Chicago students did not do as well on the English Achievement section of the Graduate Record Examination as their abilities should have allowed them to do.

Then, in 1969, several hundred students seized the Administration Building to begin The Sit-In. During those weeks and after, the English department faculty and students spent many hours reviewing the curriculum. Undergraduates objected to the heavy requirements and particularly to the anxiety-producing examination. The "context-courses" seemed to be no different from any other courses and literary historiography was a seemingly irrelevant chore. Because a substantial segment of the junior faculty and some senior faculty agreed with the general objections of the students and because the idea of requirements was being challenged almost everywhere in higher education, a student-faculty committee was charged with designing a new curriculum that would both meet the needs of the students and preserve the intellectual rigor that characterized the college.

What that committee brought forth was based on four objectives it believed a student with a B.A. in English from the University of Chicago should reach:

1. An acquaintance with and understanding of the major authors and works of English and American literature within their general historical context.

2. The ability to work independently of the confines of the classroom.

3. An understanding of how one deals with a work from a variety of approaches: historical, critical, and interdisciplinary.

4. The ability to pose a substantial question of one's own devising, to pursue an answer, and to present conclusions clearly and coherently.

The first and second objectives were to be reached partly through a yearlong independent reading project in the junior year. The student-faculty Curriculum Committee submitted a list of selections of the major works of English and American literature, including several choices and the freedom to read intensively in the works of any one author that interested the student. Students were encouraged to organize informal evening sessions to discuss the works among themselves and with faculty. In addition, each student was paired with a faculty tutor with whom he could meet as often as he and his tutor wished in order to discuss individual texts. It was originally planned that in the late spring juniors would take a comprehensive examination that would cover both historical and critical questions, but this was later changed to a series of four or five essays of about 1,500 words each on questions the students and their tutors would individually agree on. The essays would be written in a space of ten days to two weeks and returned to the tutors for comment. The students were required to perform satisfactorily in this junior program in order to qualify for the senior year.

The third objective was to be reached by requiring students to select at least one course from each of three different disciplinary areas: courses with a strong historical emphasis, courses with a strong critical emphasis, and courses dealing with interdisciplinary topics: psychology and criticism, linguistics and literature, philosophy of criticism, and so on. This requirement did not have to be met by the end of the junior year, but students were encouraged to fulfill it by then.

The fourth objective was to be reached in two-quarter seminars limited to twelve senior English majors each. Four such seminars were created, one each in the novel, poetry, drama, and criticism, topics broad enough to allow students with a variety of interests to find seminars congenial to them. During the two quarters, each senior was expected to pose a question and pursue it, to report on his progress to his colleagues, to discuss their comments with them, to write a rough draft of his conclusions, and finally to rewrite the draft into a substantial senior paper. In addition to the three-quarter reading, the three disciplinary courses, and the two-quarter senior seminars, students would take four courses of their own choosing, for a total of twelve.

In retrospect, it is now clear that the program demanded a great deal, indeed too much, of a faculty that was very busy and of students not all of whom were totally dedicated to literary studies. For some faculty, rereading the major texts in preparation for a weekly two-hour discussion with a particularly demanding student proved to be impossibly time-consuming when added to their full teaching load, to the dissertations they were directing, to their own research, to their services in a university that is largely governed by faculty committees. But worse were those cases where the student came to the tutorial unprepared and expected to be told what was in the text. The students were unable to organize themselves into an effective and conscientious discussion group, to discipline themselves to read the material in time for the discussion, in some cases even to resist putting off the reading until the week before the essay questions were set. The apparent difficulty in distinguishing some courses as primarily historical or critical in orientation made the distribution requirement suspect for some, and the apparent lack of complete success by some students in one or two of the seminars called all the seminars into question. Combined with a faculty contracting in the face of university-wide financial difficulties, these problems finally led to a decision to make what was required only elective, resulting in the current program: twelve quarter courses in English of any variety or combination.

For some students, this program was outstandingly successful. They reported that the freedom to work independently taught them to discipline themselves, that the seminars were extraordinarily helpful in their intellectual development. But for students who depended more on the formal organization of courses or who could not find a subject that could hold their interest for twenty weeks, the program was a failure.

At about the same time the program was revealing its shortcomings, faculty who once were given one-quarter course credit for advising students and approving programs had to turn over their duties to a group of well-meaning but, understandably, not always well-informed administrative advisers, because the faculty was needed to teach courses. This put the students into the hands of people who did not have any particular interest in the discipline of literary studies and who could not persuade students that some courses were important enough to select even though they might not appear to be as attractive as others. Combined with the decision to require only twelve English courses of any description, the sense of a distinct English concentration began to dissolve. Students were assigned to individual faculty members who would give advice if asked, but a minority of students consulted with them before drawing up their programs, many of which were organized almost entirely around nineteenth- and twentieth-century courses.

This growing isolation of students from faculty contact, a sense that there seemed to be no rationale behind the English concentration, and perhaps another change in the intellectual ambience of our time (few junior faculty from 1970 remain) have led to the establishment of yet another Curriculum Committee which will offer the department yet another program. Whether it will be adopted in the submitted form is difficult to predict, but there is an undercurrent of dissatisfaction with the present lack of any curricular structure.

The objectives described earlier still pertain to the new program. Others have been added. One is that we should offer distinct options that speak directly to specific, identifiable needs. For the student aspiring to graduate school (perhaps a third to a half of our population), there is proposed a "comprehensive" program. (The terminology has not yet been agreed on. We are hoping to avoid the sense of first- and second-class programs.) In the junior year, the student will take a modified three-quarter reading program. A faculty member has been assigned to organize the discussion, to invite other faculty members to speak on their special interests, and to create conditions that will insure that students keep up with their reading. Students will also be assigned to individual faculty tutors for discussion about texts and to help them construct their essay questions in the spring. It is assumed that if fewer English majors participate in this particular option, we will be able to match them with faculty members who can provide them with the assistance they need. Moreover, if a student wishes, he may substitute for the reading course two courses in periods before 1700 and two courses in periods between 1700 and 1900, an option that will further reduce the demand on faculty time for tutorials. The program will also require a student to take at least one course in the major genres of poetry, novel, and drama; one course in a major figure, ordinarily Shakespeare; and a formal course in criticism. (A single course in, say, Chaucer, would satisfy the period, poetry, and single figure requirement.)

In his senior year, the student is expected to present a research paper to the department that represents what he considers to be his best work. The paper can be written in several ways: in the senior seminars (now one quarter long and more specialized), in a reading-research course of one to three quarters in duration, or merely by substantially rewriting a paper written for a regular course. The intention is to allow the student to do research and writing that require more time and intellectual commitment than is possible in the usual one or two weeks devoted to a research paper at the end of a ten-week quarter. But it will not demand that the student unable to find an engrossing topic spend large amounts of time finding one.

A second program is the "generalist" program, a program for those not committed to graduate work in English. The generalist has the same requirements as in the comprehensive program with the exception of the required courses in criticism and the single figure. The generalist program also expects its students to present examples of their best writing, but the subject matter may be, if they wish, much less traditional. It may consist of a piece of reportage, a series of reviews of plays, films, or books, an informed interview with a local figure associated with the arts, a biographical or historical sketch, and so on—projects that require research that would take a student out of the library and into other environments for their material. He may, upon application, take up to three courses outside the English department if he can demonstrate their relevancy to his project.

A third program is in creative writing. These students have the same requirements as in the generalist program, but in their junior year, they may devote the equivalent of two quarter courses to creative writing. Their work is reviewed by a faculty committee, and if the committee accepts the student, he may devote up to three quarter courses to a senior writing project.

A fourth program is the drama/theater concentration. Students selecting this option will take three courses offered in the history of the theater, one in modern drama, and one in Elizabethan drama, ordinarily Shakespeare. In their senior year, they devote up to three quarter courses to a senior project: a play they write or one they produce and direct.

All four concentrations require a total of twelve quarter courses counted toward their concentration.

A final sentence in the description of the program qualifies the apparent strictness of these options: "Students with special interests may, with the consent of the Curriculum Committee, devise a program to meet their particular needs." In this way, we hope to solve the problem of advising by stipulating a variety of set programs, each with academic integrity, so that most students will not have to be individually counseled. But we will allow the exceptional student to submit a program of his own design.

Whether this curriculum will meet the objections of both students and faculty remains to be seen. The usual faculty objection to programs of this kind has been that not every student could be expected to produce a major senior project. By allowing a student to satisfy this requirement by rewriting a paper he has already submitted for a class, we hope to avoid demanding too much of some students; and by allowing other students to devote up to three quarters to a paper, we hope to give the enthusiastic and interested student enough room to stretch his intellect. The number of students in the reading tutorial will be significantly reduced not only by the variety of programs being offered but also by the option of satisfying the period requirements with two courses before 1700 and one in Shakespeare. The opportunity for independent work remains, but it is not required.

Throughout all the debate that has accompanied the many revisions of our curriculum, I should emphasize, none of the faculty has seriously questioned the ultimate intellectual quality of the English program. Whatever disagreement we have about the ends of a concentration in English and how to achieve them, we have always had confidence in what we believe to be the constant strength of our curriculum: the excellence of a faculty that has distinguished itself in its scholarship but still takes its teaching responsibilities with great seriousness. The quality of teaching is scrutinized by every academic body that reviews appointments and promotions. The constantly changing curriculum reflects not an indifference to undergraduate education but a common and enduring concern with it based on a variety of experiences and philosophies of education.

It is difficult to describe the general nature of the courses that have made up the curriculum because they are so varied. Except for the three-quarter reading in the junior year, which is evolving into a loosely structured formal survey of the major texts in English and American literature, the department has not regularly offered broad survey courses. A characteristic course is devoted to a single figure or combination of figures: Chaucer, Shakespeare, Milton, Lawrence and Hardy, Faulkner and Hemingway, etc. And while the subject matter courses often deal with traditional period topics such as the Romantics or the Metaphysical Poets, there are probably as many more specialized topics such as the Harlem Renaissance, American Gothic, and Modern Fantasy.

In the last few years, the number of English majors has slightly decreased, but that is probably due as much to the creation of two or three new programs in the college which appeal to students who might otherwise have chosen English as to any loss of interest in the subject matter. We do not, of course, measure our service to undergraduate education only in terms of the number of majors we have, but also by how full our classes are. By that measure, we continue to attract many students from all over the university.

Some courses, naturally enough, are less crowded than others: Old English, linguistics, bibliography. In order to make these more specialized courses available to those exceptional students interested in them, we open them to both graduate and undergraduate enrollment. It has been our experience that undergraduates easily hold their own in classes with graduate students. (And it gives the undergraduate offerings an exotic cast: not every English major in the country has an opportunity to take Middle Scots poetry.)

There are those who would like to see undergraduates do more work in bibliography, historiography, linguistics, and Old and Middle English. But infrequent attempts to require one or another of them have not been successful, so in these areas we rely more on persuasion, usually ineffective, than official mandate. On the other hand, we could fill courses in modern fantasy, modern novel, film, and so on many times over. But the limitations of a small faculty make that impossible.

Despite all these curricular changes, one principle has endured: the faculty is still as concerned with good questions as with good answers, with helping students develop an understanding of the ways to ask questions as well as a knowledge of the standard answers. We fully expect to change this curriculum again to meet those goals.

Joseph Williams
Professor of English

Courses Added in the Last Five Years
Survey of Black American Literature
Women Poets
Practical Criticism
Science-Fiction
Modern Fantasy
Poetry and Music
The Problem Novel
The Literature of Excess
Black Humor
Richard Wright and Gwendolyn Brooks

Most Popular Courses
Shakespeare
Eighteenth-Century Novel
Romantic Poetry
Late Nineteenth-Century Novel

American Gothic
Modern American Literature
Modern Fantasy
Modes of Criticism
Theory of Poetry
Theory of Drama
Modern Drama

Least Popular Courses
Linguistics
Bibliography
Eighteenth-century poetry and nonfiction
Medieval courses (except Chaucer)

Courses Most Attractive to Nonmajors
Modern literature, particularly novel courses
and single figure courses

5

Cornell University

What was once the central idea of our department—that the history of English literature is culturally important to Americans and ought to be studied systematically for that reason—has failed to connect with the present student generation.

Chairman Barry Adams
Goldwin Smith Hall
Cornell University
Ithaca, New York 14850

Full-Time Faculty 49

Calendar Semester

Type of School Private research university

Requirements for Major Ten courses (38-40 hours), two of which must be English or American literature written before 1800; two additional courses in the literature of a foreign language. No comprehensive examination.

To understand what has happened to our undergraduate curriculum in the last five years, it is necessary to sketch briefly the situation that existed ten years ago. In the mid 1960's, the department was engaged most conspicuously in the following teaching activities at the undergraduate level:

(1) Freshman English: a two-semester course in composition, with a smattering of elementary literary analysis, required of virtually every freshman from each of the seven undergraduate schools and colleges of the university;

(2) Major British Writers: a two-semester lecture-cum-discussion survey of British literature, required of all sophomores from the College of Arts and Sciences intending to major in English;

(3) an array of upperclass courses organized around the major periods and personalities of British literature, with important but ancillary components in American literature, expository writing, and creative writing;

(4) an honors program for about twenty percent of our majors, consisting of elite sections of the sophomore survey, followed by special seminars in three of the upperclass semesters, an honors essay in a fourth, and a comprehensive examination shortly before graduation.

It seems doubtful in retrospect that anyone engaged in these activities at the time could have explained them as natural expressions of an ideal curriculum. Indeed, except for the honors program, it is difficult to detect many signs of a curriculum, in any strict sense of the word. What we provided instead was a largely unintegrated succession of learning experiences, each of them (we hoped) of interest and value to our students. On the other hand, we assumed that each student, with the help of his faculty adviser, would put together a rational program of study. Moreover, there were reasonably effective checks on rampant pluralism in Freshman English, the sophomore survey, and the honors program. No doubt there were other, less easily discoverable grounds of commonality in the department of the mid 1960's. It was a much smaller department, its Ph.D. program was still modest in comparison with what it has since become, it had no M.F.A. or M.A.T. programs. All members of the faculty were more fully engaged in undergraduate teaching, and there was consequently a greater opportunity for developing and sharing those assumptions that set useful limits on diversity.

The only common assumption that was embodied in our curriculum, however, was that of academic liberalism—the assumption that once English majors had passed through their required Freshman English and their required survey of British literature they should be trusted to put together a coherent program of upperclass courses in consultation with a faculty adviser. What has happened since the mid 1960's can be perceived as a continuation of that liberal tradition, although it is possible to argue that liberalism disappeared under the stresses of the late 1960's, to be replaced by a fervent devotion to diversity. At any rate, the changes can be illustrated most graphically by chronicling the fate of those characteristic activities enumerated earlier in this narrative.

(1) Freshman English disappeared in 1967. The course was largely in the hands of assistant professors and graduate student teaching assistants, who were understandably detached from the processes by which this kind of common, required course had come into being. Many of them felt, rightly or wrongly, that the course did not really teach students to improve their writing skills. More important, they were unhappy with a course that offered little to teach or write about except writing itself. Just as these feelings were coming to the surface, the university administration became agreeable to major innovations in undergraduate

education, and in 1967 Freshman English was replaced by some 30 to 40 topically defined courses in what was for a time called the Freshman Humanities Program and is now known as the Freshman Seminars Program. Our department has consistently done between one half and two thirds of the teaching of this program, but every other department in the humanities, as well as a few outside the humanities, also participates. All courses, regardless of their departmental sponsorship, have as their principal objective the improvement of writing skills. But each course is also designed to introduce freshmen to an academic discipline and to provide them with a taste of the small-class experience.

During its first three or four years the Program was a great success. Freshmen were exhilarated by the range and variety of courses from which to choose, and many faculty members, working together with teaching assistants, entered into the spirit of innovation. Most of the new courses were simply more interesting than Freshman English had been, and the process of planning and experiment by which the new courses came to exist had the effect of improving our attention to freshman education in literature and writing.

By now much of the spirit of innovation has gone. The most successful courses have been institutionalized, and to the present generation of students and younger faculty the Program is simply part of the established way of life at Cornell. New freshmen courses continue to be invented from time to time, but too often the invention seems forced by pressure from those who are committed to maintaining the spirit of innovation. Moreover, those faculty members (many of them from outside the English department) who opposed the Program from the outset on the grounds that it would fail to teach our students how to write are now claiming more and more vociferously that their prophecy has been fulfilled. Perhaps it has. Certainly we have upperclass students who cannot write very well, just as we had in the days of required Freshman English. The causes of this condition seem to us endlessly debatable. In any event, the chief defenders of the Program have shifted their ground, and we hear more talk about the virtues of a small-class format than about the best means of teaching students how to write. The individual sections of the various courses, each limited to twenty students, continue to provide that seminar-like experience which is felt to be so important for young people entering a large and impersonal university.

For the past three years, the English department has operated a noncredit tutorial service—the Writing Workshop—for freshmen requiring more intensive practice in writing. Whether the Workshop will develop into tomorrow's innovation in undergraduate education at Cornell remains to be seen; at the moment we are forced to regard it as an experimental project.

(2) The sophomore survey required of prospective English majors came under attack in the late 1960's. Some faculty members, particularly those teaching the discussion sections, objected to the format of the course. Others objected to its status as the only approved entry into the English major: alternatives should be available, they argued, for those students who wished to prepare themselves in some other way for upperclass study of literature. Touched by this appeal to liberalism, the department opened an alternative path to the major, one that included, among other things, an ahistorical close reading course in poetry. The other things soon disappeared, but the poetry course worked out very well and was eventually joined by similar courses in fiction and drama. More recently, the sophomore course in creative writing has been added to the list, and we now have four alternative prerequisites from which a prospective major must choose at least one.

The format of the sophomore survey course was also changed by eliminating the unifying lecture. Within a few years of this development, the course lost its standing as one of the approved entries into the major. It still exists (ironically, in a format resembling that of a decade ago), but principally as an elective for sophomores from all corners of the university. So far as the English major is concerned, then, we have in effect decided that the cultivation of literary and critical skills is a more important preparation than knowledge of a literary tradition.

(3) We continue to offer a wide range of upperclass courses, and it is still possible to detect the historical organization that prevailed ten years ago. But American literature and creative writing now exist on the same footing with the British literary tradition. There are more courses than there were ten years ago, and the student majoring in English has, if anything, even more freedom to put them together into an upperclass program of study. The department has always declined to specify the courses necessary for completion of a degree with a major in English; it has said only that a major must complete at least eight upperclass courses in English, and it has always explicitly allowed at least two of these eight to be waived in favor of advanced courses in comparative literature, a foreign language, or some other comparable experience which makes good educational sense to a student's adviser. It was always assumed that the two-semester sophomore survey would naturally suggest to students how to create a sensible program of literary studies in the upperclass years. When that assumption was challenged by the facts, there were various attempts to institute some kind of distribution requirement. Although most of these attempts have come to nothing, we have recently established a requirement that two of a major's courses must include English or American literature written before 1800.

We also require that all our majors do the equivalent of two years' college-level work in a foreign language. This requirement is of great antiquity and seems never to have been seriously threatened. In the last five years it has been questioned several times, partly on the grounds that it discourages substantial numbers of students from majoring in English, but it has always been defended vigorously by the majority of our departmental colleagues.

(4) The honors program has almost entirely disappeared as a result of revisions undertaken over the past five years. With its advanced sections of the sophomore survey course, its special seminars in major authors and literary periods, its fifty-page thesis, and its comprehensive examination, the program seemed to many of our colleagues too much like a graduate program. There was also criticism of the program from those who disliked the elitism of a tracking system in a college that was already highly selective in its admissions policy. From about 1967 the components of the program were gradually stripped away or altered beyond recognition, until today it is only the thesis that survives—and it survives only as one of several options available to students who wish to graduate with honors in English.

The old honors program, however, was at least indirectly responsible for one of the most significant changes in the department to take place in the past ten years. Until about 1965 almost the only way for an upperclass English major to experience a genuine advanced seminar was to become an honors student and take the three prescribed honors seminars. The department then set about making this experience available to all its juniors and seniors. It created some 15 or 20 such seminars, in a variety of relatively specialized topics, and threw them open to all upperclass majors who were able to meet the prerequisites established by the instructor. As an educational development, this was seen at the time as comparable in importance to the introduction of the Freshman Humanities Program. Of course it required a sizable increase in our teaching staff, but in the late 1960's this was no problem. We simply grew, along with the rest of the profession, and by 1970, when we first heard cries of budgetary restrictions, we found ourselves with about fifty-five regular faculty members, most of them heavily engaged in teaching these small, valuable, but no longer elitist seminars for juniors and seniors.

In this atmosphere of relative freedom, many of our majors are turning to American literature in a way that tempts us to predict that before long the defining center of our undergraduate teaching activities will be the American rather than the British tradition. It is noteworthy that the more popular American literature courses are by no means all seminar-size courses; evidently, the attraction of the subject in this case outweighs the value of the small-class experience.

Students are also flocking to the creative writing workshops. These are offered at every level except the freshman, and although it is theoretically impossible for a student to complete an English major with writing courses alone, a few of them manage to build a concentration in writing at the expense of literature.

Courses in modern fiction consistently draw large numbers of students; those in modern poetry are somewhat less popular. From among the more traditional courses, only those in Shakespeare, regardless of format and level, do a very brisk trade. Our teacher-preparation program (for prospective teachers of English at the secondary level) is small but growing. We have never wished to invest heavily in this kind of preprofessional work at the undergraduate level, but it appears that student interest may force us to reconsider our position in the next few years.

Barry B. Adams
Chairman, English Department

Scott McMillin
Director of Undergraduate Studies

Courses Added in the Last Five Years
Readings in English and American Literature
Introduction to Drama
The Art of the Essay
Theory of the Romance Form
Children's Literature
The Psychoanalytic Tradition in Literature and History

Courses Dropped in the Last Five Years
Twentieth-Century Literature
Studies in American Literature
Literature of the Negro Experience in America
British Literature
Honors seminars

Most Popular Courses
Creative Writing
The Reading of Fiction
American Literature
Shakespeare

Least Popular Courses
Specialized topics in English literature before the nineteenth century (except Shakespeare and, sometimes, Chaucer)

Courses Most Attractive to Nonmajors
Modern Literature
Creative and Expository Writing
Shakespeare

Courses Most Attractive to Majors
Modern Literature
American Literature
Creative Writing

Major Changes in Curriculum
The survey requirement for majors has been dropped; the prerequisite course has been changed to one term of analytical and critical techniques in literature or one term of creative writing.

6

Duke University

[The present undergraduate curriculum] seems to represent stability in departmental offerings and confidence on the part of the faculty that they know what they can do.

Chairman Louis Budd
Duke University
Durham, North Carolina 27706

Full-Time Faculty 31

Calendar Semester

Type of School Private research university

Requirements for Major 24 hours, six at the sophomore introductory level, 12 in historical periods of which six must be a two-semester survey course, three in a major author, and three unspecified. No comprehensive examination.

The English department at Duke University consists of 31 full-time faculty members (15 professors, 12 associate professors, 4 assistant professors), three part-time lecturers, and 35 graduate tutors. With the exception of the Director of Graduate Studies, and one or two full professors on rare occasions, all of these staff members teach undergraduate classes. The number of majors in the department has been approximately 250 for the past several years, between five and six percent of the entire student body of Trinity College of Arts and Sciences.

The usual class size at the junior-senior level is limited to 40 students; the class size at the sophomore level is limited to 28 students; the class size at the freshman level is 15 to 17 students; the class size in the freshman composition conference is one. (The average class size in the upper level courses is, perhaps, 30 and 25, respectively.) During each academic year the department offers seven different semester courses at the freshman level and seven at the sophomore level; at the junior-senior level the department offers all of its undergraduate courses during a two-year cycle, but most of its courses it offers every year—about 60 semester courses.

The undergraduate major at Duke has remained constant at its center during the past twenty years while shedding more and more of its fringe qualities. In 1955 the major consisted of a six-hour sophomore survey of British literature (Major British Writers), 18 hours at the junior-senior level, six hours at the senior-graduate level, and 18 hours of "related work" in other departments in the humanities. The sophomore survey included Chaucer, Shakespeare, Milton, and Donne in the first semester; Pope, Fielding, Wordsworth, Keats, Dickens, and Yeats in the second. The first semester of this course has been virtually unchanged in those two decades; the second has suffered minor substitutions of one author for another. On the whole, however, this introductory course has been and still is a constant in the program of the major. The 24 hours at the upper level were distributed according to a pattern of requirements designed to expose the student (1) to three divisions of literature in English: British before 1800, British after 1800, and American; (2) to a major author—Chaucer, Shakespeare, or Milton; and (3) to a single period of literature for a study of comparatively greater "depth"—i.e., two semesters. These 24 hours were to be undertaken at the junior-senior level and at the senior-graduate level. The six hours in the senior-graduate courses offered the student a smaller class with more intensive work than was customary at the undergraduate level (or so it was thought). The related work was drawn from appropriate courses in esthetics, art, English education, foreign languages and literatures, history, linguistics, music, and philosophy.

In 1964 the first of a series of changes from this scheme took place. The requirement of six hours in senior-graduate courses was deleted; in place of these courses, elective "Conference Courses" were instituted at the undergraduate level to provide the same small and intensive kind of class that had been available at the higher level. These courses were and still are very popular. They have, in effect, removed the seniors from the graduate classes—and so sharpened the focus of those classes—and they have made available to staff not approved to teach on the graduate level the opportunity to teach in this particular kind of class. The number of hours required at the junior-senior level then became 24. In 1969, when the total number of hours required for graduation was reduced in the college from 124 hours to 96, the department reduced the number of hours required at the junior-senior level from 24 to 18. At the same time the principle of related work was dropped.

In the fall of 1974, the department revised the major again, increasing the number of hours at the junior-senior level from 18 to 21, and requiring nine hours in the three divisions of literature in English, three hours in "a major author" (redefined to include American authors and authors from later British periods), and three hours to be taken—after advising—in any courses in the department (Writing, Linguistics, Literature in Translation, Speech and Theater, Criticism, or Literature).

Though the department concentrates on a major program in literature and in literary history and criticism, it offers other areas of interest that do not lead to a major. The largest of these is Speech and Theater (11 semester courses). The speech courses serve students aiming for public positions in politics, law, and the ministry. The forensics courses serve those interested in the law and in the undergraduate debating team. The broadcasting courses interest those working in the student radio station. The theater courses interest those in the Duke Players; they serve also as part of the newly established Program in Drama.

Creative Writing (6 courses) offers a small but popular and highly successful program in training students who wish to develop their skills. The instructors are all faculty members who have published poetry, fiction, or nonfiction in the professional world and who also are qualified to teach courses in literature and literary criticism alongside their "noncreative" colleagues. The department policy has been for many years that the best creative writers are found in those students who study literature first and their own writing second.

Foreign literature (6 courses) used to be a popular area, but a rejuvenated Classics department and a new Comparative Literature Program have caught the student fancy at our expense. It seems likely that we shall discontinue some of these courses.

Linguistics (3 courses)—one course in theory (taught in rotation by instructors from various departments), one course in history of the English language, one course in modern grammar (designed for students going into teaching in the secondary schools, but admired by others)—is a small, but sturdy, offering.

The department also provides the opportunity for independent study in one course each semester of the junior and senior years. Since few students take many of these courses, the number of independent study programs each semester varies between five and fifteen. Two courses provide the normal method of securing graduation with Distinction in English, but students can achieve this honor by outstanding work in any class during the senior year. Distinction is awarded on the basis of a long paper, prepared during this year.

Offerings for nonmajors specifically are two only. These form a sophomore survey in American literature (6 hours) and parallel the survey of British literature, but they are deliberately designed to accommodate the nonmajor. (They are not a part of the major program.) Not many years ago we offered seven or eight sections of this survey to nonmajors of every sort. It was quite popular; majors were excluded, and, hence, nonmajors found the competition not so keen as in other courses in English. It was an extremely useful course for premed students. In recent years, however, the requirements of the college have changed, and the course is no longer cited by the Duke Medical School as a course specifically recommended. The demand for the course has, naturally, decreased. Nonmajors tend also to elect upper level courses in Shakespeare, in contemporary American literature, in the American novel, and in drama. By policy of the college, one third of the places in each class is reserved for nonmajors. We always have, therefore, some nonmajors with our majors in each class.

The department also offers, more or less as "service courses," the following courses which form no part of the major: Freshman Composition and Introduction to Literature: Studies in ——.

Freshman Composition is the course designed to fulfill the college requirement in English Composition. Entering freshmen are excused from this course if they achieve a score of 700 or above on the CEEB English Composition Achievement Test. (Entering freshmen who score 3, 4, or 5 on the CEEB Advanced Placement Program test are given 3 hours credit in Humanities; they are not excused from the Composition requirement.) The course is a high enterprise in the three traditional methods of instruction: lecture, discussion, conference. Once a week the freshman class in crowds of 250-300 hears a lecture on composition or literature; the general lecturer is a member of the senior professorial staff. Once a week the freshmen in groups of seventeen attend a discussion class on the subject of the lecture or of the reading assigned; the instructor is a graduate student with a master's degree. Once a week the freshman attends a private conference (20 minutes) with his instructor in which the student's weekly theme is analyzed, discussed, and graded. We have found this method of instruction a most effective way of teaching composition.

The "English 20's series" replaces the old second semester of Freshman Composition with a varied table of elective courses in the genres. Though designed for freshmen, these courses are often filled with upperclassmen who value the small group experience (fewer than 15 students) and the unusual topics that often appear in Special Topics. These topics may include Science Fiction, Utopian Literature, Political Novels, the Wilderness in the American Novel, the Literature of the Discovery of America, and so on. The courses are offered each semester; the Special Topics offerings are constantly varied.

Courses may be initiated by any member of the department. Courses offered in the "20's series" and in the "180's"—Seminars and Conference Courses—are approved by the Supervisor of Freshman English or by the Director of Undergraduate Studies. New courses to be offered on a continuing basis are approved by the entire department (and then allowed by a committee of the college). Perhaps because it is so easy to offer a course as a seminar or conference (i.e., as a nonce course), faculty members have not been enterprising to offer new and exotic courses. Of the 17 new upper level courses instituted in the past five years, two have been created at the request of outside agencies and 14 are extensions of courses already in existence. Only one is genuinely new, the course in Criticism, erected to meet student requests. Since its creation, the course has not been popular, and as its work can be duplicated in the 180 slot, we shall probably discontinue it next year.

Courses discontinued are few in number, eight at the upper level. These have all been dropped for the most humdrum of reasons. The department has in recent years declined to approve a series of new courses leading to a major in criticism and a new course in film. The result seems to represent stability in departmental offerings and confidence on the part of the faculty that they know what they can do.

George Walton Williams
Director, Undergraduate Studies in English

Courses Added in the Last Five Years
Freshman seminars on various genres and
special topics
Advanced Creative Writing
Introduction to Linguistics
Sixteenth-Century Literature
English Drama
Twentieth-Century English Literature[1]
Canadian Literature (in English)
European Literature
Independent study courses
Criticism

Courses Dropped in the Last Five Years
English Composition (second semester)
European Literature
Technical Communication
Satire
Oral Interpretation

European Epic Tradition[2]
The Agrarian Spirit/The Industrial Spirit[3]

Most Popular Courses
Contemporary American Literature
Shakespeare
Milton
British Drama; European Drama
Contemporary British Literature

Least Popular Courses
Sixteenth-Century English Literature
Eighteenth-Century English Literature

Courses Most Attractive to Nonmajors
Shakespeare
American Literature
American Novel

[1]Three-quarters of the way through the century, we thought it not too daring to add this modern course.
[2]A special course created for the president of the university, not continued after his retirement.
[3]Two courses taught jointly by English and History. Discontinued for reasons of difficulty in staffing.

Major Changes in Curriculum
For the major, the 18-hour requirement of appropriate courses from other departments was dropped when the overall college requirement was lowered from 124 to 96 semester hours.

7

Finch College

Flexibility has helped us to make the most of our resources. . . . We developed flexibility through necessity, but we would retain it above most other qualities by choice.

Chairman Carol A. Hawkes
Finch College
52 East 78th Street
New York, New York 10021

Full-Time Faculty 3

Calendar 3-1-4 (3 terms of different lengths)

Type of School Private liberal arts college

Requirements for Major Thirty-six hours, including one senior studies seminar in either English or American literature. No comprehensive examination.

Problem: To redesign the English curriculum at a small liberal arts college in New York City. Degree requirements no longer mandate freshman English and a year of humanities; patterns in majors are changing; the budget is tight. The department has a strong will to live, but it is also afflicted with principles. How can it, with no more than the staff of three full-time and five part-time faculty remaining after budget cuts, build and teach a curriculum that will not only interest students but serve their long-term needs, a curriculum flexible yet coherent and academically sound?

This is the problem we have been facing at Finch College during the past five years. We know we are not alone. Most English departments have had comparable problems, varied, of course, by differences in size and institutional context. Our solution is still in progress, but we think we have a good framework. Despite the demise of freshman English and required humanities, we have been able to maintain our enrollment: we still serve more students than any other department in the college, we rank first among academic departments in number of majors, we have the lowest rate of attrition. At the same time, we believe we have held to standards: our majors who enter graduate and professional schools have found themselves well prepared.

When the tide of falling degree requirements swept away our comfortable base in freshman English and humanities, our curriculum was organized along traditional historical lines. We offered survey and genre courses in English and American literature. Our only major figure course was in Shakespeare. We had one course in composition beyond freshman English; it was called Advanced Writing and emphasized the writing of fiction. We called ourselves the Department of English and Comparative Literature, but there was no major in comparative literature and only three courses, a survey and two others, counted toward an English major. Our major program, like all academic majors at the college, culminated in a senior seminar, which could be elected in either English or American literature. We participated in no interdisciplinary or interdepartmental courses or majors. We had experimented with one nontraditional course called Communications '70, taught by guest lecturers from various communications fields. The idea was interesting, but for various reasons the course was felt not to be academically feasible and was not repeated.

We had then a staff of six full-time faculty. The squeeze began after the demise of freshman English, when we were no longer permitted to bring in a full-time replacement for anyone who moved on or retired; one member left that year and our chairman retired. The next year a college task force, charged with containing the recession already felt by most small, private institutions, recommended further cuts across-the-board. We lost one more full-time member, but since we still had a high enrollment our part-time staff budget was increased to allow us to continue offering all but a single course. We approached curriculum revision with a department very differently constituted, however; with so few full-time members we faced problems in advisement, continuity, and stability as well as in the curriculum itself.

To assess the situation realistically, we attempted to analyze our patterns of enrollment, the fields of competence of our faculty, and additional resources available at the college and in New York.

Enrollment. We found that we were serving at least three distinct groups of students among our majors. First, there were the academically oriented, who planned their major with the intention of entering graduate programs in English.

This was a small but important group (20 to 25 percent of the majors) including many of our ablest students. They elected more courses in English than in American literature, had a higher than average interest in period courses, and populated the senior seminars. They needed substance and also experience in critical approaches and independent study and research. Second, there were the career oriented, who tended to plan their major to satisfy interest in an aspect of the subject related to a professional or vocational field. They were attracted to drama, fiction, and writing courses with a view to work in the theater or in writing, publishing, and advertising. We had also a steady registration of students majoring in elementary education with a minor in English; they elected the surveys of English and American literature, Shakespeare, and courses in the novel. The career oriented comprised about 40 to 45 percent of our majors and minors. Third, we enrolled a substantial number of liberal arts students in the traditional sense, those seeking self-development and a heightened awareness from a major in literature. Almost 40 percent of our majors might be classed in this group. These students showed strong interest in modern literature, in genre courses (especially drama and fiction), and in studies of major authors. They responded well to cultural opportunities in the city: theater, films, poets' readings, exhibits, etc. Besides these groups within the major we enrolled a large number of students for whom English was an elective. Their choice of courses was not strikingly different. Like the majority of majors they preferred modern literature to the earlier periods, drama and fiction to poetry. Some registered for courses they felt were related to their major (Shakespeare for a major in theater arts, the modern novel for a psychology major). Some, often with the encouragement of their major departments, sought help with their writing.

Faculty. The three remaining full-time members of our department had, by combined luck and design, three separate areas of competence. One was best qualified in English literature, one in American, one in comparative. Obviously, we could not think in terms of "coverage." The three fields, however, suggested a way to improve continuity and stability. It had long been department policy at Finch for every member to teach at every level, freshman as well as senior. If we continued that policy and each of us taught intermediate and advanced courses in the field of specialty culminating in a senior seminar (our normal load is 3 courses per semester), we would have the basis for three relatively stable sequences and the advisement to complement them. Whether comparative literature could become a major in itself would depend on whether we could make interdepartmental arrangements. In all three fields of literature and in writing courses we could, through careful recruitment of part-time faculty, increase the capability of the department.

Additional Resources. The small size of Finch makes it easy for departments to communicate. Now more than ever we felt that this was needed. A comparative literature major was only one possibility we might develop through cooperation. We began to make known our interest in interdepartmental and inter- and multi-disciplinary courses, programs, and majors.

New York City, too, might offer more resources than those we had traditionally made use of in the theater, libraries, and museums. We began to think of possible student internships for the career minded and of credit for work/life experience. The college, we knew, was beginning to explore opportunities for interinstitutional exchange. If this could be arranged it would provide important additional options for our students.

We thus began to see a curriculum with varied patterns of coherence to serve the needs of major and nonmajor students; with sequences (though not broad historical coverage) in English, American, and comparative literature under the direction of full-time faculty; with additional courses in literature and writing taught by adjunct faculty; and as many academically justifiable options as we could provide.

One preliminary remained. While accepting our own basic responsibility for developing the program, we wanted to involve our students directly. We did this in three ways: discussion meetings for majors and nonmajors, informal talks with individuals and official talks with the elected departmental representative to student government, and a questionnaire. The questionnaire asked for expressions of interest in subject areas and types of courses, invited suggestions for new courses and general comments and suggestions, and included a major/nonmajor check-off. We promised to tabulate and announce the results, together with our intended response. We were prepared to weight the results against the ultimate evidence of registration figures. We knew from experience that student "demand" for a course this year may evaporate before the course can be offered next year. Still, we were prepared to keep our promise to take the results seriously.

In general the questionnaire confirmed our analysis of enrollment and student interest patterns, especially in the preference for modern literature, fiction, and drama. One thing we learned—and this was three years ago—was that interest in writing courses had begun to grow. We could not undertake, as some requested, a program in journalism, but we were encouraged to add electives in writing. Interest in literature in translation was also high and supported our idea of an interdepartmental comparative major.

We came up to the point of revision, therefore, with a good foundation to build on. In general we followed the pattern that had taken shape during the process of assessment. Some of our specific decisions may be of interest, as well as the patterns that have emerged.

The Basic Sequences. The English major at Finch, like most other academic majors, requires thirty-six credits (usually 9 4-credit courses) for the student working toward the B.A. In English and American literature we retained the survey and the required senior seminar for the beginning and end of the sequence. Between these we offered sixteen genre, period, and major figure courses at the intermediate and advanced levels, seven to be available every year, the rest on an alternating basis. From our old curriculum we retained, with revisions, courses in the novel, in modern drama, and in Shakespeare. We added Black Writers, and in alternate years Studies in English and American Writers (since the topics chosen for these would be different each year, students could elect them more than once). We eliminated or combined old courses that overlapped. The effect was one of streamlining and responsiveness rather than radical change.

In writing we initiated more new courses. To help students with specific writing problems (more nonmajors than majors here) we offered a freshman level Writing Workshop. That was for the fall term, to be followed in the spring by the Writing Conference, a series of individual tutorials for students who needed further help. From the beginning we had to hold down registration, especially in the Conference. Individual instruction seemed to appeal to students, and they responded well. We used the Conference also to provide short-term help without credit to students referred to us by other departments.

At the intermediate level in writing we offered Writing about the City, which sent students to observe and write about aspects of life in New York. It was reportage rather than journalism in the technical sense and held possibilities for coordination with courses on urban topics offered by the government and sociology departments. A year later we added a more advanced course in Critical and Investigative Writing. Both of these courses were taught by professional writers who joined our part-time faculty. To replace the old Advanced Writing course we offered Writing Drama and Fiction. This coordinates with genre courses in literature and with work in theater arts. Like the other writing courses it is taught by a professional who comes to us part-time.

All writing and literature courses are supplemented by a program in independent study which was adopted on a college-wide basis at about the time we revised our curriculum. A student with some previous competence in a field may, with permission, pursue a project independently for two or four credits in any term. Since only full-time faculty are expected to advise such students, we have been obliged to limit the numbers, but the program increases opportunities, especially for majors. We have also arranged internships for qualified students in publishing and public relations. So far this has been on an individual basis, but we may extend it.

Interdepartmental and Interdisciplinary Cooperation. We talked with our colleagues in foreign languages and arranged an interdepartmental major in comparative literature. It followed our major pattern of thirty-six credits but had to be planned as a coherent study of relationships between two or more literatures. At least a year's work had to be completed in a foreign literature in the original language, and at least sixteen credits in comparative literature courses including a senior seminar. The foreign language requirement has proved an obstacle to students but is an essential that cannot be abandoned. The comparative literature courses we have added to our own curriculum serve also to enrich the English major. Since period, genre, and major figure courses are offered by the foreign language departments, we built a twelve-course alternating sequence on concepts of tragedy and comedy, myth and archetype, and comparative drama and fiction.

While we were arranging the comparative literature major, the history and government department arranged an interdepartmental major in American Studies, including our courses in American literature. The theater arts department agreed to give major credit for our courses in drama and for Writing Drama and Fiction. Psychology gave major credit for our new comparative literature course in Myth and Archetype. A number of course "clusters" were identified, cutting across departmental lines, on such topics as the city, Black studies, and the Renaissance. All departments agreed to urge students to plan work allied with the major: at least twelve credits at an intermediate or advanced level in a related field. English majors have tended to do allied work in history, psychology, or art history. Since English relates to most other disciplines, the department has drawn many students electing literature as an allied field.

English has cooperated in two interdepartmental courses, Perspectives on Women and Perspectives on Film. Although these do not count toward the major, they have strengthened our relationships with other departments and have increased our students' options.

External Programs. In addition to internships and other career opportunities, interinstitutional exchange has become an important supplement to our curriculum. Finch now has exchange agreements with five other institutions, four of them in the city. So far we have not used exchange on a broad scale, but it provides an opening we need.

To describe a curriculum and how it came into being is not like seeing it in operation. Its parts are a little like the centipede's feet, which work best when he does not think about them. The fact is that our curriculum at Finch has worked well for us and our students for three years now. If we had to name one quality that has helped us most, it would be flexibility. Flexibility has helped us to make the most of our resources, to serve students of diverse needs, to increase our options through cooperation. We developed flexibility through necessity, but we would retain it above most other qualities by choice.

Carol A. Hawkes
Chairman, English Department

Courses Added in the Last Five Years
The Writing Workshop
The Writing Conference
Writing about the City
Writing Drama and Fiction
Critical and Investigative Writing
Black Writers in America
Studies in American Writers
The Renaissance
Jacobean and Restoration Drama
The Age of Elegance: Studies in Pope, Swift,
    and Thomson
Studies in English Writers
Modern Poetry
Independent Study in English
The Tragic Vision
The Comic Experience
Myth and Archetype in Literature
Studies in European Writers
The European Novel
The Makers of Modern Drama
New Directions in Theater
History of the Theater

Courses Dropped in the Last Five Years
Approaches to Literature

*Incorporated into other courses.

Communications 70
Advanced Writing
Theater and Mankind
Oral Interpretation of Literature
English Drama: 1590-1890
Modern American Fiction*
Modern English Poetry*
Modern American Poetry*

Most Popular Courses
The Writing Conference
Writing about the City
American Literature
Modern American Drama
The American Novel
The Modern English Novel
Great Russian Writers
All independent study offerings

Least Popular Courses
Courses that require study of earlier periods of English literature and/or reading other than drama and fiction, e.g., Jacobean and Restoration Drama, English Literature of the Seventeenth Century, Victorian Literature

Department Offerings: Majors and Nonmajors
A larger percentage of majors than nonmajors had, in a study made a year ago, a strong interest in English rather than American literature; majors were inclined toward study-in-depth of major authors while nonmajors inclined toward the surveys; majors were interested in writing fiction and poetry and nonmajors in journalistic writing.

Major Changes in Curriculum
Freshman English has been dropped as a requirement; English majors are no longer required to take the survey course.

8

Fisk University

The department is growing more rapidly than at any previous period.

Chairman Rosenteen B. Purnell
Fisk University
Nashville, Tennessee 37203

Full-Time Faculty 10

Calendar Semester

Type of School Private liberal arts college

Requirements for Major 33-38 hours, including Survey of English Literature, Survey of American Literature, Advanced Composition, Shakespeare, Milton/ Chaucer, one period course, one genre course, one Black literature course, one senior seminar. Comprehensive examination required.

The primary assumption of the English department at Fisk is that students should be offered an expanding range of options. Our program, then, is neither traditional nor ultrarevolutionary. It aims to assess realistically the needs of and possibilities for the students whom we serve: namely, the variety of patterns of living available and the students' ability to negotiate successfully the environmental and personal factors that confront them.

Our program serves two major functions: to the student who is not an English major it offers the literary experience and discipline inherent in a liberal education; to the English major it offers the professional knowledge and skill necessary for a career in teaching, for graduate studies, or for preparation to enter fields such as law, communications, and interdisciplinary studies of various kinds. For both majors and nonmajors the department has provisions for specially designed programs with emphasis in Black literature. English courses, except the Senior Seminar, special seminars, and tutorials, are open to all students.

As a contribution to the general education of the Fisk student, our department offers basic courses in writing and literature, in communications, which combines the emphases of reading, writing, listening, and speaking, and in fine arts, which combines literature, music, and art. In writing and speaking, our approach is bidialectal to the extent that students are exposed to a variety of patterns of expression through a consideration of the appropriateness or effectiveness of the particular usage for the occasion or desired ends. In literature, the multiethnic approach is also followed, through which the idea of the universal man is tested. Through our interdisciplinary courses we consciously explore the interrelatedness of ideas, concepts, and modes as viewed from the perspectives of several disciplines.

Support services are available in writing and reading skills development through the English Department Center for Intensive Instruction in Writing Skills, remedial and developmental, and in the University Reading Center. These reinforce class efforts and provide extensive and more personalized opportunities for working on more resistant problems.

Certain courses offer opportunities for internships in radio, television, and newspaper publishing. These not only provide experience in the "real" world, but enhance career goals and opportunities. Communications and Mass Media, for example, is one of the most popular courses and is growing in scope and influence at the university. The primary reason for its success is its skillful combination of theory and practice: students do not have to wait until they get a job beyond college to learn what things (such as grammar, punctuation, accuracy in reporting or judging) are important; they see this immediately. The end result is that they, many times, ask us for various types of learning experiences, which may be handled individually or as a group.

In the nonmajor program, then, the aims of the liberally educated person are pursued. The question of values, life-styles, and alternative patterns in all areas is explored against a background of a developing awareness that one's ability to *choose* is posited on one's being prepared for many possibilities or eventualities. For example, one can choose to use so-called "Standard English" or other patterns only if one knows each of them. This approach has, I feel, done much both to facilitate our teaching of more traditional English and to unleash a healthy vitality and creativity in our courses. The flexibility inherent in this approach has done wonders to improve faculty morale and commitment. Students at Fisk find English one of the most attractive departments.

For the English major, our course offerings reflect the same general concern for pluralism as those of the nonmajor while still retaining broad professional training. We therefore offer survey courses in the areas of American (which includes Afro-American), Afro-American, and English literature; author courses in Chaucer, Milton, and Shakespeare; period courses in each leading period of English literature: Renaissance, Neoclassical, Romantic, Victorian, and Twentieth Century; and genre courses in prose fiction, poetry, and drama. In addition, we offer a writer's workshop, for creative writing emphasis, three courses in African literature, Introduction to Linguistics, Writing for Secondary Teachers, and free elective seminars. The content of the seminars is determined by the instructor and reflects his interest in literary problems that lie outside of regularly offered courses. Seminars are intended to offer an opportunity for intellectual creativity and adventure for both student and instructor by examining new problems of literary scholarship and criticism or by reexamining old ones. More recently, our seminars have reflected the departmental interest in interdisciplinary studies. As such, they have provided a vehicle for both interdepartmental and intradepartmental developments with great possibilities, besides stimulating both English faculty and majors to engage in primary research and establish contacts with leading persons and centers of learning in the region. Some of the recent courses of this nature are the Oral Tradition, the Afro-American Experience as Reflected in Literature, Art, Music, and Folklore, and Communications and Mass Media.

The department also offers the Senior Tutorial for independent study. Under the supervision of a selected instructor, the tutor and tutee work out an individualized program of reading and research according to the student's particular career or professional goals. Though individual programs differ, it is expected that the reading be extensive and wide-ranging in the first semester leading to a final paper that will see a heterogeneous body of material in a significant theoretical light. The readings of the second semester are limited and culminate in a fully researched paper on a topic approved by the tutor. Only five senior majors are selected each semester to take this course. A grade point average of B or above is required.

The English Program at Fisk continually examines and reexamines its program offerings to gauge its effectiveness and institutes such changes as are indicated. Recently, we reinstituted the senior examinations (involving a written, oral, and research paper) as a requirement for graduation because it was determined that our majors demonstrated little carryover from course to course, and possibly not beyond their major study. The examination further gives us a better view of our shortcomings in offerings and in instruction. As a consequence of the examination we discovered that an earlier assessment of our major potential was indicated. This year we instituted a sophomore review in which students who had declared an English major were examined, not as a requirement for departmental admission but for diagnostic purposes. The examination results are reviewed by an assigned adviser and, subsequently, the adviser confers with the student on activities and a program to effect a sound and adequate major experience. This procedure prevents the discovery of major problems at a point when remedy is impossible.

The department is growing more rapidly than at any previous period. It has vitality and a healthy sense of itself, of where it is and of where it wants to go. The staff is totally committed to providing a sound educational experience for its students and toward faculty growth and development. We cannot guarantee in advance a "finished product," but we do evaluate constantly what we do and recommend and institute change as needed.

Rosenteen B. Purnell
Chairman, English Department

Courses Added in the Last Five Years
Communications
Communications and Mass Media
The Afro-American Experience as Reflected
    in Literature and Folklore
The Oral Tradition
Masterpieces in World Literature

Courses Dropped in the Last Five Years
Introduction to African and Afro-American
    Literature
Survey in World Literature
Honors courses

Most Popular Courses
Black literature

Shakespeare
Folklore
Other interdisciplinary courses

Least Popular Courses
World Literature
Chaucer

Courses Most Attractive to Nonmajors
Shakespeare
Folklore
Black literature

Courses Most Attractive to Majors
Victorian Literature
Shakespeare

Major Changes in Curriculum
Requirements for the English major were introduced. Before these requirements became part of the curriculum Shakespeare was the only specification in the English major.

9

University of Florida

We have gone with our strengths and have increased those strengths where we could.

Chairmen Richard Green
Ward Hellstrom
University of Florida
Gainesville 32611

Full-Time Faculty 66

Calendar Quarter

Type of School Public research university

Requirements for Major Regular Major: forty-eight hours, including one course in English literature before 1800, one course in literary theory, criticism, or genre, and one course in the study of language or the practice of writing. No comprehensive examination.

The University of Florida is a rather unusual university in that all its colleges and professional schools are located on one campus; that is, agriculture, law, and medicine as well as fifteen other colleges and schools are located in Gainesville. It is unusual also in that *all* students in their first two years go into University College, a college with a dean and six departments. At the end of the sophomore year, students who have satisfactorily completed the general education requirements of University College are awarded an Associate of Arts degree and apply for admission and transfer to one of the upper division colleges or schools. As a result of an articulation agreement between the State University System and the Division of Community Colleges, graduates from any of the twenty-nine public Florida Community Colleges are also allowed to transfer to any of the nine universities in the State University System. The result is that the plurality of students in the College of Arts and Sciences, for example, are from Florida community colleges and not from University College.

Another peculiarity is that our collegiate structure has provided this university with two English departments, each with its own chairman and its own faculty—one in University College and one in Arts and Sciences. Since 1972 we have been in the process of bringing the two departments together into one. Though we are still paid on separate budgets and have two chairmen, we are in all other respects a single department: we hire as one, make committee appointments and teaching assignments as one, and so forth.

The Lower Division

Over the past ten years, freshman English expanded from one basic three-quarter freshman English course, which taught composition as well as some language study, some speaking, and an introduction to literature. A quarter course in language study was added, one in contemporary reading, one in special topics, one in film (later divided into 2 quarters). We had always had separate sections of the basic course for honors students. (Innovations in curriculum were often tried in honors sections and later adopted in the general sections.) The basic course was restructured about four years ago: the first quarter became a rather cursory survey of various genres with some composition. The student in the winter and spring quarters then chose from introduction to fiction, introduction to poetry, and introduction to drama; or from one of the courses in language, contemporary reading, special topics, or film.

This past year we changed the curriculum again. We offer only five freshman courses now: 109, a course we do not teach but give credit for on the basis of the CLEP exam; 111, the first quarter of freshman English, strictly composition, no literature; 121, 122, and 123, introductions to fiction, drama, and poetry. In the winter we will add 124, The Rhetoric of Film, a composition course using film to teach composition. All other courses originally offered as freshman courses have been raised to the 200 level to attract nonmajors, though they are open to freshmen as well. I should say here that freshman English is no longer required (as of 1973-74), though students must take nine quarter hours of some English some time in their four years to satisfy general education requirements. In practice most freshmen take freshman English courses at least in their first two quarters; by their third quarter they are likely to be confident enough to take a sophomore or upper division course.

We have found that raising four courses from the freshman to the sophomore level has considerably increased the enrollment of nonmajors in them: slightly more than thirty percent of their enrollment are students above the freshman year. In all, we teach twenty-two sophomore level courses including the traditional English and American Literature survey courses, world literature courses, and college honors courses. We have inherited two library science courses taught by library people. We have introduced this fall two creative writing courses (one in fiction and one in poetry) at the 200 level and an introduction to Shakespeare at that level. The creative writing courses filled early and the Shakespeare course registered ninety-six the first time offered. (We hope to make this a large lecture course.)

The Upper Division

We teach, though not each quarter, 29 courses at the 300 (junior) level and 38 courses at the 400 (senior) level. Of the 67 courses, ten are writing courses (4 creative writing, the rest expository and such); four are courses in language; three are in film; one in teaching in the secondary school; one is an honors seminar; 50 are literature courses—21 surveys, 15 genre, four individual authors, ten special topics. Of these literature courses 18 are British literature, six are American literature.

Writing Courses

The demand for creative writing courses always exceeds our supply of instructors. This is partly because creative writing is popular on most campuses and partly because our program is a particularly strong one. For some reason enrollment in poetry sections has fallen off slightly in the last year.

Business communications is one of our most popular courses. We teach about 24 sections a year with a total enrollment of 400. Our enrollment is down some 20 percent from a couple of years ago when the course was required by the College of Business Administration, but now state requirements for accountants will increase that enrollment. We are confident of the course and hired a second specialist in it this year. We are also planning to hire a specialist in technical writing next year and hope to expand our work there. The College of Engineering wants an additional 125 students per year taught a specialized course in technical writing.

Demand for advanced exposition and argumentation is up partly because so many students are aiming at law school. We teach about four sections a term. We can and would like to build those courses up.

Language Courses

In all we offer six undergraduate courses in language. We are somewhat short of linguistics; so we have not expanded our offerings, but we should.

Film Courses

Film study has exploded since we introduced the first film course at the freshman level in 1969 and at the junior level in 1970. Last year film enrollment had increased 837 percent over that of 1969; we taught 35 sections of four courses with a total enrollment of 1,769. We could have taught many more. This year we will teach six different undergraduate courses in film and next year add a seventh. (Enrollment will continue to increase in film studies, which will probably become a part of an interdepartmental film division, but the English department will contribute the history and criticism of film.)

A number of things should perhaps be said about film study. (1) English departments are the logical places for history and criticism of film courses to develop. English teachers are more skilled at criticism than speech, communications, broadcasting, or a host of other departments that might wish to appropriate film studies. It is not a simple thing for one skilled in literature to retrain as a specialist in film studies but it is certainly possible. There has been a good deal of interest in film in our department and specialists in other areas have spent the last three years preparing themselves to teach film courses. (2) There is a real danger of letting serious, rigorous study degenerate into courses in going to the movies. We have tried to be extremely careful about the rigor with which our teachers are trained and with which the courses are taught. (3) Film courses are costly but not prohibitively so. Careful selection of films for purchase and for rental can reduce costs considerably. (4) Film study really needs a coordinator of some kind to insure that film orders do not overlap and that there is coherence in the program. With all the problems, film study is well worth investigation by English departments not already engaged in it.

English in the Secondary Schools

We are trying to build enrollment in this precarious course. Students do not get credit for it toward secondary certification because the College of Education will not allow substitution for their methods courses. We have established a secondary school committee in the department, which has begun visits to high schools and middle schools in order to determine how we can better prepare secondary school teachers. We have begun in the last two years to take this responsibility very seriously, a responsibility ignored by this department (and most English departments) for a long time.

Literature Courses

We still offer most of the traditional British literature courses by historical periods, including a Medieval course, three Renaissance courses, three Restoration and eighteenth century, two Romantic, two Victorian. In addition, we teach three English novel courses, one course in Chaucer, and two in Shakespeare (plus one at the 200 level). We have dropped courses titled Milton and Spenser and teach those figures in a variable course called Renaissance Studies. Enrollment in these courses has dropped steadily in the last five years: between 1969-70 and 1973-74 enrollment dropped by 34 percent.

We have a similar attrition in American literature courses. Between 1969-70 and 1973-74 enrollment in traditional American literature courses at the junior and senior level dropped by about 48 percent. Some people in American literature feel that the change from American surveys to American major figures and themes and movements put students off.

There are apparently a number of other reasons for the attrition in enrollment in traditional British and American literature courses: (1) we changed the major requirements, no longer stipulating a number of specific traditional courses for majors. While we still required some British period courses and Shakespeare from the major who did not expect to go to graduate school, we ceased in 1970-71, the year of greatest attrition, to require American literature at all. (2) In 1970-71 we added an upper division film course and ethnic literature for the first time. Together they enrolled 365 students, but over one third of these students were neither majors nor even in Arts and Sciences. Still, some who might have taken

British or American literature may have been drained away into the new English courses. The question is, would they have drained away into non-English courses if we had not begun to expand offerings? (3) Surely many students who may have had teaching careers in mind have had their dreams aborted by the job market and have not continued in traditional programs leading to graduate schools.

Rather traditional world literature courses that we have offered for years tend to draw about the same number of students they always have.

One of the most popular literature courses is Children's Literature. We teach about 600 students a year in it, mostly elementary school majors but also pediatric nurses, child psychology students, and others. Large enrollments are occasioned by the course being required by elementary education, but enrollment is growing because we are establishing a good children's literature library, have added writing for children to our creative writing program, and have hired a specialist in children's literature (and we are looking for another). We hope children's and adolescent literature will become a significant part of what we do.

We have only this year hired two folklorists and we will continue to build and expand our work in folklore. We expect it to interest majors and to appeal to nonmajors from anthropology, education, and other fields.

The new genre and criticism courses we have added seem to be popular but it is rather early to tell. They are not radical courses: forms of fiction, forms of drama, forms of poetry—and our old theory and practice of modern criticism.

The other new courses we have added—Afro-American Literature, Jewish Literature, Women in Literature, and Science Fiction—look as if they will do all right as well. There is no question about science fiction; we have tested it for two years and it strikes us as a valid and even necessary pursuit for an English department. Women in Literature is more in doubt; we have had to cancel it a number of times because of underenrollment. Afro-American Literature and Jewish Literature are as yet unknown quantities.

The Major

We have radically changed our major requirements over the past five years. We have gone from requiring 24 out of 36 hours to requiring only eight out of 36 with these eight hours to be chosen from a large selection of alternatives. We now require 36 hours at the junior level or above with one course in English literature before 1800 and one course in literary theory, criticism, or genre. Admittedly, this requirement is not very stringent but we wanted to allow the student who wished to do so to prepare in writing or in language studies, rather than in literature. The department has tried to protect itself from charges of simply turning students adrift by developing an elaborate advisement system. We have an advisement room with a library of materials on careers for English majors and an advisement booklet that outlines useful courses and programs for preparation in five separate areas of concentration for majors—in literature, linguistics, creative writing, film, secondary teaching. It also recommends courses and programs that would be appropriate for students preparing for law school, medical or dental school, pharmacy, business careers, technical writing careers, communications and allied fields, or those simply wanting a sound liberal education.

Conclusions

All members of the department are not equally happy with what we have done in the last few years. We have not innovated simply to gain enrollment. We teach only those things we respect and regard as valid scholarly or service pursuits. By and large the department thinks we are on the right track. This fall, university enrollment increased by slightly more than ten percent; so did enrollment in English. If we follow the same pattern as last year, English will add to that ten-percent increase in winter and spring quarters over the same quarters a year ago.

We feel confident that we are serving our students, the state, and our discipline. My feeling is shared by most of my colleagues, I think, that if we had it to do over again, we wouldn't want to do it differently. We have gone with our strengths and have increased those strengths where we could. Our faculty have been willing to try things and to educate themselves in areas new to them. What it all comes down to, really, is that the best curriculum in the world won't work without a good faculty. We are fortunate that ours is bright, energetic, and cooperative.

Ward Hellstrom
Chairman, English Department

Courses Added in the Last Five Years
Renaissance Studies
Elementary English
Expository and Argumentative Writing
Introduction to Shakespeare
Use of Books and Libraries
History of Books, Printing, and Libraries
Beginning Poetry Writing
Beginning Fiction Writing
Introduction to Film
The Forms of Fiction (Drama, Poetry)
Afro-American Literature
Jewish Literature
Women in Literature
The Movies as Narrative Art
History of the Film
Argumentative Writing
Analysis of Propaganda and Techniques
Anglo-Irish Literature
Studies in Literary Genres
Modern Science Fiction
Medieval English Literature

Courses Dropped in the Last Five Years
Spenser
Milton
Elizabethan Drama
Survey of American Literature
Victorian Writers

Least Popular Courses
Introductory British literature surveys
Introductory American literature surveys
Senior level period courses in British
    literature

Most Popular Courses
Introduction to Film
Business Communication
Creative Writing—Fiction
Film as Narrative Art
History of Film
History of the Language
Chaucer
Shakespeare
Children's Literature

10

University of Kansas

The department has just undergone an unprecedented, massive review and revision of its curriculum with a particular view toward rationalizing its course offerings.

Chairman George Worth
University of Kansas
Lawrence 66044

Full-Time Faculty 51

Calendar Semester

Type of School Public research university

Requirements for Major At least twenty-one hours of junior/senior level courses in English and one course outside the department. Major British Writers to 1800, Major British Writers after 1800, Shakespeare, Major Author course, period or genre course in British literature before 1900, elective numbered over 500, course in American literature, course in British history, art, or philosophy, or a course in relevant European cultural history. No comprehensive examination.

The department, consisting of 51 full-time and some 85 part-time teachers, of-fers over 70 courses which are principally designed and scheduled for undergradu-ate enrollment. The majority of these courses are intended to respond to the needs of three broad areas:

i. Service to the university
   (A) Freshman-Sophomore Requirement
      1. A three-semester sequence of composition-literature courses with in-creasing emphasis on literature as the student progresses through the sequence. The retention of a nine-hour sequence for this purpose indicates the university's recog-nition of the need for beginning students to have ample training in writing and in the critical reading and interpretation of reasonably sophisticated texts. The reten-tion of this unusually strong requirement also signals the confidence of the univer-sity as a whole in the ability of the department to produce and sharpen those skills.
      2. At the instigation of the department, the College of Liberal Arts and Sciences now allows a student to substitute a course in a genre (i.e., short story, novel, drama, poetry) or a survey (Major British Writers i and ii, Major American Writers) for the third course in the required sequence.
      3. A two-semester honors sequence for superior freshmen fulfills the same requirement described under (1) above. This pair of courses recognizes the re-duced need of the superior students for basic training in writing and critical skills and provides at the same time a degree of difficulty and competition.
   (B) Courses heavily used by students in the School of Education
      1. Some courses have been especially designed to fulfill specific needs of students who are working for teaching degrees, although they retain general use-fulness and interest for other students as well.
         (a) Literature for Children (required for elementary education majors)
         (b) Introduction to the English Language (required of secondary edu-cation majors)
         (c) Advanced Composition (required of secondary education majors)
      2. Other courses, such as Major British Writers i and ii, American Litera-ture surveys, and Modern English Grammar, although less obviously designed with education majors in mind, are considered very useful in the training of public school teachers and are part of the requirements for the B.S. in Education and the certification process in the state of Kansas.
   (C) Technical writing courses are offered principally as a service to students in engineering, and a new course in scientific writing is designed to respond to the general need of students in other fields, such as business and prelaw.

ii. Courses that can be taken to fulfill general graduation requirements or chosen as electives
   (A) A number of courses on the sophomore level may be used to fulfill the College of Liberal Arts and Science's distribution requirement in the humanities. These are "introductory" courses to the various genres and survey courses empha-sizing major authors in both British and American literatures. Classes are kept small, the atmosphere is reasonably informal, and some emphasis is placed on developing critical skills through both discussion and the writing of critical papers. These courses enjoy tremendous popularity, and the department has been unable for years to accommodate all students who wish to enroll in them.
   (B) A full range of creative writing courses is arranged in three levels of diffi-culty: the first level is open to freshmen and sophomores, the second to juniors and

seniors, the third only to those who can prove some competence in at least one of the areas of creative writing by submission of fairly accomplished manuscripts.

(C) The remaining undergraduate courses are all open to nonmajors as well as majors. They range from broad background courses (e.g., The Bible, The Classics, and Modern Literature), through courses of broad but generic emphasis (The Comic Spirit, The Tragic Spirit, etc.), to particular types of literature (Folklore, Science Fiction) and specialized topics (Black American Literature, Women and Literature). Major authors courses (Shakespeare, Chaucer, Milton, which have their own, regularly offered rubrics, and a Major Author course which changes title and subject every semester and is often offered in several different sections, such as Twain, Dickens, Whitman, Browning, Faulkner) provide an essential part of the major curriculum while at the same time enjoying broad general appeal and subscription. A full sequence of period courses, in which the modern periods of literature lead in the quantity of courses, frequency of offering, and enrollment, and courses in literary criticism and philology round out the offerings of the department.

III. Courses principally designed for majors in the department

While the department does not discriminate between those students who wish to go on to graduate school and others, the requirements for the major are structured in such a fashion as to make possible the judicious selection of courses for preparation for graduate school.

(A) Those students who wish to go on to graduate school will most likely fulfill the major requirements by emphasizing British and American literature survey courses, taking the fullest possible advantage of the broad range of period courses, and selecting major authors courses whenever they fill a gap in their preparation for the specialized demands of advanced study.

(B) For the superior students among the majors, the department offers a number of honors courses which are offered in limited enrollment seminars on special topics. Directed reading and research is also available, and students who are qualified and wish to graduate with the formal designation of Honors in English must write an honors essay which is directed by a specialist in the area of the student's interest.

(C) Although students who are not interested in study in English beyond the B.A. degree must fulfill the basic requirements for the major, they may leaven their program by taking any of the other undergraduate English courses.

(D) The most recent innovation in the major program is the availability of a creative writing major which allows a student to divide his time evenly between creative writing and literature courses.

Although the outline given above, together with a list of courses, may give a prospective student a decent overview of what the department has to offer, it unduly emphasizes the requirement and service aspect of the curriculum. It fails to reflect the pervading attitude of the members of the department and plays down the flexibility of the curriculum and the consequent freedom of choice for the student. Hence, a few general remarks may be in order.

There is no rigid classification of courses to distinguish between majors and nonmajors. Practically all courses are open to both, and a class consisting of all English majors is a great rarity. Prerequisites have been kept to a minimum: students are encouraged to seek information and advice about the courses and are then allowed to find their own level. A liberal "drop/add" policy makes it possible for students to change their programs when they encounter unexpected difficulties.

The department has just undergone an unprecedented, massive review and revision of its curriculum with a particular view toward rationalizing its course offerings: number, level, sequence, content considerations were raised and discussed by a plethora of volunteer committees, overlapping in their interests and involving every member of the department. The result, coordinated by a curriculum review committee, has been a reduction of the total number of courses, establishment of clearer relationships among courses, elimination of overly specialized courses, creation of greater flexibility by the expansion of categorical "topics" courses, and better response to student interest by all these means.

A large number of topics courses has allowed the department to offer many unusual and special interest classes without having to "carry" specific courses for each in the catalog. Thus, the course The Literature of —— has recently been offered in the incarnations of The Literature of Violence and The Literature of Baseball. Both versions enjoyed full academic respectability and broad appeal.

Although it is too early to come to any firm conclusions about the efficacy of the new curriculum since it has been in operation only one academic year, it seems clear that some of the new courses in modern literature and some courses with new approaches, such as the course on Women in Literature, are enjoying good success and hold considerable promise for the future. The only outright failure in course offerings has been a two-semester, five-credit sequence of the British literature survey which was specifically designed for prospective graduate students. It was abolished in the curriculum revision.

In order to make course choices by students more intelligent and reliable, the department issues, well in advance of enrollment, a brochure containing the description of each course, written by the instructor, in which he or she indicates the particular approach to be taken, lists the required reading, specifies the number and type of examinations to be given, and describes any other written work required.

Above all, it should be emphasized that the department, though large and demonstrably dedicated to scholarship and research, prides itself on its commitment to teaching and personal contact with students. Nor is this pride a mere pious protestation: since the inception of a series of programs for recognizing outstanding undergraduate teaching at the University of Kansas a decade ago, the department has had more than half a dozen winners and many more finalists in the various competitions, in the ones conducted exclusively by students as well as in those administered by faculty committees.

Gerhard Zuther
Associate Chairman, Department of English

Courses Added in the Last Five Years
Middle English
Studies in the English Language
English Literature I and II
English Literature Supplement I and II
Science-Fiction
Sources and Analogues for American and
    British Literature
Studies in ——
Introduction to Short Story
Women and Literature
American and British Poetry since 1945
American English
Scientific Writing

Courses Dropped in the Last Five Years
Ideas in Mid-Victorian Literature
American Short Story
English Literature Supplement I and II
Studies in Criticism
Special Studies in Modern Drama
British Prose of the Nineteenth Century

Most Popular Courses
Major British Writers I and II
Literature for Children
Shakespeare
The British Novel from Beginnings to Jane
    Austen

The British Novel from Scott to Hardy
The Modern British Novel
Major Author: ——
Topics in American Literature
Science-Fiction
Modern American Drama
Various creative writing courses

Least Popular Courses
Upper division classes with narrow emphasis
    on a specific phase or period
Medieval literature—exclusive of Chaucer—
    where students must master Middle
    English

Courses Most Attractive to Nonmajors
Literature for Children
Science-Fiction
Shakespeare
Creative Writing
The Literature of ——

Courses Most Attractive to Majors
Major British Writers I and II
Shakespeare
Major Authors
Creative Writing
Topics in American Literature
British Novel to Jane Austen

Major Changes in Curriculum
A broader offering of courses and several of more current interest are available since the de-emphasis on training of students for graduate study. However, the curriculum still offers courses to meet the needs of the graduate school candidate.

11

Michigan State University

*We often advise our majors to take work in economics, business, or public affairs.
So that we may be apprised of the job situation, the Associate Director of the
Placement Bureau sits ex officio as a member of our Curriculum Committee.*

Chairman Alan Hollingsworth
Michigan State University
East Lansing 48824

Full-Time Faculty 46

Calendar Quarter

Type of School Public research university

Requirements for Major 48-57 hours, with requirements differing according to
three options: preprofessional (for careers in English), English Education, and preprofessional (for careers other than English). A creative writing concentration is
possible under any of the three emphases.

Until 1968, like most good university English departments, we treated our undergraduate English majors as though their main interest was, or should be, graduate study. To be sure, like many other departments, we had made some allowances for diversification. We had agreed to staff an English methods course (located in the College of Education), we had developed a strong sequence in language study which covered both philology and applied linguistics (including TESOL), we offered an impressive *bloc* of creative writing courses, and, because of the varied talents of our faculty, we provided—beyond the traditional program in English and American literature and literary criticism—a rich collection of courses in comparative literature and methodology, American studies, and contemporary literature. But quite clearly, our undergraduate major was centered on the traditional program of preprofessional courses that assumed, or implied, future graduate study, preferably study leading to the Ph.D.

The Development of Emphasis II

Six years ago we took the first significant step in recognizing the heterogeneous nature of the department's undergraduate English major population. We had before us the fact that although some sixty-five percent of our majors were planning to teach English in high schools or middle schools, there was little acknowledgment of this intention in our courses. Several years earlier we had, indeed, recognized an important student need when we agreed with the College of Education to establish a position jointly appointed for the teaching of English methods. But this action had not had much consequence in curriculum. It had not led to the development of a program in English Education, and this is what sixty-five percent of our majors needed if they were to meet their responsibilities as teachers (especially in the light of the then recent Dartmouth Conference) and if they were to become leaders in the profession.

We began our efforts to change our program by visiting local high schools and middle schools and talking with teachers, students, and principals. We visited superintendents of schools, directors of curriculum, and directors of personnel. We read the appropriate journals and wrote to and telephoned the appropriate people. We came to believe that we needed a new course specifically for the teaching of writing to younger people, a course that would provide extensive weekly field experience in the schools over a long period of time so that our teaching majors might learn how they could help younger people write well. We already had an excellent course in advanced writing to help university sophomores and juniors improve their prose (English 213: then Intermediate Composition, now Writing Workshop) and were at that moment in the process of bringing into being our new freshman writing course (English 101: Responses through Writing/English 102: Writing and Composing). We needed something else specifically for our prospective future teachers. Since no one in the department felt equipped to design such a course beyond a sketch, and also because whoever came to us to develop such a course would have a whole program to create and direct, we made a vigorous national search for leadership in this area. Our search was successful, one consequence being that nowadays *English Journal*—the central publication in the field of English education—is edited in our department, another being the development of such courses as Literature and the Adolescent, English Field Experience Internship, and Teaching Competencies in English. A further consequence has been the achievement of some reputation as a department providing national leadership in yet another area, as evidenced by three Gull Lake conferences on the teaching of English, one cosponsored by MLA, one cosponsored by NCTE, and one cosponsored by the Michigan Middle Cities School Association.

Meanwhile, another new kind of course was emerging in the department, a course that arose out of our experience visiting the schools in the interest of teaching writing. This new course was in the teaching of reading, a course not often found in a university department of English. Our course soon came to be based on psycholinguistic, linguistic, and applied linguistic insights and associated with the humanistic tradition of "language experience" and literary criticism. This course, English 408 (The Teaching and Learning of Reading in the Context of Other Language Processes), is now five years old and has given rise to English 408-B, 408-C, and a graduate course, English 847 (Reading and the English Teacher), taught jointly with the department of psychology. English 408 is based on insights drawn from linguistics, literary criticism, and psychology, and also from experience in the schools. It, too, is a field experience course. A secondary English major in our department works in the schools a part of his sophomore year in the teaching of writing, a part of his junior year in the development of materials and teaching strategies, and a part of his senior year in the teaching of reading. Such experience in the field is in addition to practice teaching and whatever school experience is involved in English Methods as well as in such courses as American English.

The Development of Emphasis III

Three years ago we took the second significant step in diversifying the major in recognition of the increasing heterogeneity of our actual and potential English major population. In a year that ranks as one of the most remarkable in the long history of the department's curriculum, the department diversified its major into three "emphases," it added a new *bloc* of popular culture courses, and it made an important proposal to the university in general education.

The diversification into three "emphases" was, in part, a consequence of a study of what English minors and especially what nonmajors and nonminors elected when they had the opportunity. As difficult to establish and sketchy as such information proved to be, we saw enough to believe it worth our while to attempt to gain majors out of minors and other students who were choosing to take many courses in English. We also saw reason to work harder to attract nonmajors to our offerings and to invite students to consider the numerous career possibilities in English other than in teaching. Helpful advice came to our Curriculum Committee from an officer of the university's Placement Bureau, who joined the committee as a member and who still sits on the committee. Good advice came also from two large corporations that make much use of English majors in their respective operations: Sears Roebuck and Company and IBM. And very useful advice came from undergraduate majors and minors and nonmajors who liked our courses. Thanks to such help we broadened the base of this option. As a part of this option, in addition to courses in popular culture, we increased our offerings in folklore and mythology, restored our old world literature courses, created a course in Literature and the Film, and, more recently, developed a course in Women and Literature. This option also involves a choice of "cognates" drawn from many places in the university.

It is worth noting that the establishment of the popular culture sequence followed a procedure very much like that which brought the English education program into being. We sketched the courses we thought we needed and simultaneously conducted a vigorous national search for someone who might provide leadership in the area. As before, our search was successful; as before, our new colleague helped us define and establish the new courses during the year before he actually moved to our campus. Thus we could start the new program when he arrived, thanks to his guidance.

As the third part of our remarkable year, in response to a strong drive conducted by our provost for reform in general education on our campus, the department—with the approval and support of the Dean of the College of Arts and Letters—proposed a set of collaborative efforts with various strong departments on the campus to improve the quality of undergraduate writing. For example, the departments of chemistry and English might join in offering a year course in writing. English 213 (Writing Workshop) would constitute the first quarter of work. The two departments might team teach the second quarter of the course and thus learn much about the needs and talents of each other. Chemistry might be responsible for teaching the third quarter; we would help if needed. Our pattern of collaboration with the department of physics or the business college, or other interested parties, might take a different form, though we think of English 213 as a constant in the equation. Such a set of liaisons would make the maximum use of our English 213, one of the most popular courses in the university, the demand for which we can never seem to satisfy. The course would serve as a catalyst in helping the whole university community solve a mutual problem in the quality of undergraduate writing.

The Strengthening of Emphasis I

Whereas Emphasis II and Emphasis III may help the traditional major program stay alive (it seems quite lively at the time of this writing), without the traditional major program the other two would soon wither. All three are essential to the collective enterprise. The first prepares certain students for graduate work and affords an excellent liberal education to those for whom that is a sufficient goal. The second makes our secondary English teachers highly competitive in this state and in other states. The university Placement Bureau (as of this writing) believes our secondary education English majors are at least holding their own in the contest. The third affords career possibilities in English or in English plus a given minor, or set of minors, to those who are not adequately served by the first two. But it, too, provides a good liberal education. As the number of traditional majors in Emphasis I diminishes, Emphasis III helps to stabilize our total enrollments with both new majors and nonmajors, which, of course, helps us to retain positions vacated by retirements and to continue to offer a rich and complex curriculum. The loss of any one of the three emphases might well lead to an abruptly simplified teaching program and a very different way of life for all of us.

Alan Hollingsworth
Chairman, Department of English

Courses Added in the Last Five Years
Responses through Writing
Introduction to the Study of Literature
    I and II
Composition for Secondary Teachers
Introduction to Popular Culture
Popular Literary Forms
Major Themes in English and American
    Literature
Playwriting
Literature and the Adolescent
English Field Experience Internship
World Literature in English
World Literature in English Translation
Genres and Themes in World Literature
Studies in Popular Culture
Women and Literature
Literature and Film

Most Popular Courses
Writing Workshop
Masterpieces of American Literature
Shakespeare
Problems in the Teaching of Reading
Problems in the Teaching of Reading and
    Writing

Teaching Competencies in English
Literature and the Adolescent
English Field Experience Internship
Composition for Secondary English Teachers
Introduction to Fiction
Introduction to Drama
Introduction to Poetry

Courses Most Attractive to Nonmajors
Contemporary Literature
Masterpiece sequence
Forms of Literature sequence
All writing courses
Literature and Film
Popular Culture

Courses Most Attractive to Majors
Writing and Composing
English Education sequence
Period literature courses
Chaucer
Milton
Shakespeare
American and Contemporary Literature

12

Northern Arizona University

In revising our old curriculum we set out to eliminate as many requirements as possible, and in their place we substituted a program which insists that all courses teach essential principles and none serve merely as preparation for an important educational experience somewhere further down the line.

Chairman Max James
Northern Arizona University
Flagstaff 86001

Full-Time Faculty 31

Calendar Semester

Type of School Public comprehensive university

Requirements for Major Thirty-five hours, including Major Principles in the Reading of Literature and nine hours in one of the following Primary Sequences: English Literature, American Literature, Comparative Literature, and Creative Writing. Six hours in one of two Secondary Sequences: Folklore and Linguistics or one of the literature sequences not chosen as the Primary Sequence. No comprehensive examination.

The department curriculum committee, which began revising our undergraduate and graduate offerings in the fall of 1970, set for itself the goal of creating a curriculum that would be at once flexible and carefully structured. We accepted as true the proposition that faculty teach better when they have wide latitude in creating course plans and that students learn more easily when they are given freedom in choosing courses and programs. We acknowledged that a curriculum must be tightly structured if it is to provide what the student needs and what society and our profession expect him to receive, but we did not feel that our sense of professional responsibility was incompatible with student demands for relevance, interest, freedom of choice, and flexibility. To implement these two objectives we devised a sequential organization of our offerings that allows maximum freedom of teaching methods and selection of materials within individual courses, but also provides strong impetus toward specific educational goals.

Our curriculum is divided into six sequences: English Literature, American Literature, Comparative Literature, Creative Writing, Folklore, and Linguistics. There are sequences such as literary criticism and popular culture inherent in the curriculum which have not yet been formally designated, and others that can be created with minor changes and additions. The way the sequences function to provide our programs with both freedom and direction can best be understood through a description of the literature sequences. The foundation course for all three literary sequences, and the only course required of all majors and minors, is Major Principles in the Reading of Literature, a practical criticism course that gives majors the basic critical principles and writing skills they need in later courses. Each of the literature sequences begins with a sophomore Issues course. The purpose of an Issues course is to delineate cultural and literary issues that distinguish the literature of one tradition from all others. To achieve this, the instructor organizes his class around a central issue which underlies the whole of the tradition, e.g., American Culture and the American Literary Tradition: The Years of Discovery, the Years of Change. Enough works are chosen—masterpieces as well as lesser works—from early and recent writers, and themes are broad enough to give the student a good sense of what one looks for when reading in this tradition. The emphasis in the comparative Issues course is on the study of the literary problems the reader has in responding to literatures outside his own cultural sphere. In this sense it functions as a course in criticism. However, it is organized thematically and, when dealing with Continental topics, outlines issues that set Continental literatures apart from the Anglo-American tradition.

Sophomore Issues courses are followed at the junior level by Topics courses. These courses, such as The Noble Man, The West and American Literature, The Tragic View of Life, are also organized thematically, but the focus is narrower, reading materials are drawn from a shorter time span, and some directed research is expected of students. The sequences are completed at the senior and graduate levels by Readings courses and Authors courses. For seniors, Readings and Authors courses augment the materials and approaches of the Issues and Topics courses; for the graduate student weak in an area, they serve as an abbreviated sequence, providing first a survey of key issues and representative works and then an intense study of one or two writers. In addition to the basic four, in each area there are corollary classes which flesh out the sequence. For example, the English sequence can be augmented by Major Issues in Ancient Literature, Introduction to Shakespeare, and Readings in Medieval Literature.

Throughout the literature segment of the curriculum, the emphasis is upon developing awareness of central literary principles and the ability to use basic reading and writing skills. In addition to creating an awareness of the key cultural and literary patterns within a tradition, an Issues course gives the student the perspective needed to discover such patterns for himself. Through close readings of key works, extended class discussions, and critical essays, the analytical talents developed in the introductory criticism course are reinforced. Topics courses extend and deepen the cultural insights gained in the Issues course, and they introduce students to the perspectives necessary to do research in the field. Readings and Authors courses cover the same critical skills in essentially the same order as the Issues and Topics courses, but in a much more intense manner. At this level students are introduced to the concepts necessary for extended analytical and research projects. The genre courses, Modern Drama, The Nature of Poetry, The Nature of Short Fiction, and The Nature of the Novel, along with Problems in the Reading and Presentation of Literature and Literature, Culture, and the Human Personality, develop analytical precepts from perspectives different from those of the Issues-Authors sequences. Throughout the literature courses, however, the emphasis is on creating those insights and abilities that allow students to read sensitively, responsibly, and confidently on their own and to write about what they have read with equal awareness and control. The development of reading and writing skills cannot, of course, take place in a vacuum. Students must read extensively and they must develop a strong historical sense, but we feel that students who only know *about* literature, who must rely on others for their critical judgments, have received only part of an education.

Most other areas of the curriculum work according to the same organizing philosophy that governs the literature offerings. For instance, in English Linguistics the student interested in language is given an understanding of the basic principles that govern the scientific study of language. This course is followed by English Grammars. As a senior the student might take Dialects and Current English Usage. By adding another five courses as a graduate student, he can acquire a substantial training in linguistics.

The sequence is not only the organizing principle of our offerings, but it is the means of structuring the degree programs. After Major Principles in the Reading of Literature, the student is expected to focus his work through three courses in one sequence and two in another. The only other English requirements for the B.A. or B.S. are one of two senior criticism courses, Problems in the Reading and Presentation of Literature or Literature, Culture, and the Human Personality. In practice, most students take more than the minimum nine hours for their major sequence, and some students take nine or more hours in several sequences.

One area in which the sequence concept is not applicable is the Liberal Studies program. At Northern Arizona, university-wide requirements are made up of special courses which only nonmajors are allowed to take. Though the sequence concept is not appropriate here, our five Liberal Studies offerings, Masterpieces of World Literature, Folklore, Introduction to Shakespeare, Understanding Literature, and Literary Expressions of Underground Movements, have been structured according to the same philosophy that governs the rest of the curriculum. If anything, the principle that orders our majors courses is more crucial to the designing of courses for nonmajors. A class for students who may never take another English course should emphasize truly important literary concerns. Students with a passing interest in literature, as well as majors, want to know why people read, why people write, what makes some works good and others bad, and what parts of the human personality result in artistic expression. Answering these fundamental questions, at least as much as that is possible, and helping students to enjoy materials they might otherwise never experience are our chief aims in classes for nonmajors.

An issues oriented curriculum provides both freedom and control where they are most wanted. Instructors are free to concentrate on the materials that most directly develop major concepts and skills. In turn, students are free to take those courses most relevant to their interests and career objectives. But if the curriculum allows considerable latitude in relation to course content, it carefully defines the kinds of skills each course is to impart. Because all courses are organized to develop basic issues and skills, there is no need for elaborate program require-ments. Implicit in an elaborate list of requirements is the assumption that only in some courses will students learn important concepts. What, then, one wonders, are the other courses doing? In revising our old curriculum we set out to eliminate as many requirements as possible, and in their place we substituted a program that insists that all courses teach essential principles and none serve merely as preparation for an important educational experience somewhere further down the line. Though we recognized the usefulness of general guidelines, our ideal has been to create a curriculum in which every course deals so directly with major concerns that, even if a student were allowed to choose courses on a purely random basis, he would still receive a meaningful education.

In addition to the freedom and built-in structure it provides, our curriculum has several other advantages over our old program. Since the instructor is not obligated to cover a specific block of material, he can build his current interests into his classes, there is more class time for discussions, and students are freer to pursue independent reading and writing projects. Since the institution of the new curriculum, student and faculty morale has improved. Advising sessions go better. Students appreciate the fact that offerings and requirements are part of an articulated philosophy. The curriculum's orientation toward the student is as responsible as any single factor for the fact that, in spite of the weak job situation for teachers, the number of declared majors is holding steady. Students who return to us after trying other majors express appreciation for the vitality of our courses and the realism of our programs. Students who were planning to teach in high school reorient their programs toward other career goals and remain in English rather than shifting to other departments.

Though the sequence approach tends to insure that each course carries a strong sense of purpose and each sequence a strong impetus, it does not automatically guard against duplication of works and themes. To insure that ma-terials are not repeated within two courses of a sequence during the time required for a major to pass through the program, each sequence is overseen by a committee of that area's instructors. To insure that all classes work together to form a coherent program, instructors submit detailed course proposals to the department curriculum committee. If two instructors request the same course or sequence, the committee chooses the proposal with the sharpest sense of purpose and the strongest command of the materials. Prior to the advising period, the approved course descriptions are distributed to students and faculty. In this way everyone in the department has a clear sense of what each instructor will be doing in his courses for the next term. Of all the things we do to insure continuity in our offerings, the publication of course descriptions each term is probably the one most fully appreciated by our students.

The publication of detailed course descriptions is but one manifestation of the change in perspective the institution of this curriculum has necessitated. In essence, what we have done is shift responsibility for program continuity from curriculum requirements to the teachers immediately responsible for a term's offerings. For instance, much of the responsibility for the continuity of the student's program now lies with his adviser. From the outset we have realized that without a consistently strong advising system, the curriculum could not work. Our advising may not yet be all it should be, but individual instructors and the department as a whole have put considerable effort into making advising contacts work for the student. Rather than force each student to follow mechanically a rigid set of requirements constructed for the average student, we help him construct a program as close as possible to his own interests and career objectives. A curriculum so flexible that sections of the same course can have entirely different readings and focuses makes it possible to create a special major for each student.

It is this flexibility and responsiveness to the individual, we feel, that has made it possible for us to weather the present professional crisis. The fact that the curriculum can be made to function along so many different axes has allowed us to respond quickly to new opportunities. For instance, the fact that our technical writing sequence is defined in broad, open-ended terms has made it relatively easy to enlarge the program severalfold without adding a single new line to the catalog. The catalog description reads, "Development of advanced skills in technical report writing for teachers as well as professionals in technical fields." We are able, with this broad description, to offer a separate section of this course each term for each of five majors: forestry, geology, technology, police science, and prelaw. In the near future we will have sections for students in premed and the social sciences. The program continues to expand—in fact, the writing sequences are the programs in which the nonmajors show the greatest interest—because we are willing to tailor sections to the specific needs of other departments. Because the whole curriculum is oriented to present the student with basic experiences, we have been able to construct new Liberal Studies courses that have won easy approval by a cautious university committee and quick acceptance by nonmajors. For instance, our new Folklore course drew 150 students the first time it was offered; this is a strong enrollment, even for a Liberal Studies course. Because the curriculum defines a teaching *process* that holds true for all courses rather than defining blocks of information, it is possible for us to create complete new programs without disturbing the curriculum's balance. We are in the process of creating two new sequences, an undergraduate complement to our graduate ESL program and a composition sequence for students interested in writing careers in business and government. Both these programs will dovetail nicely into existing offerings.

Our new curriculum has more than lived up to our original intentions, but not everything has been as successful as we could wish. The health of this program is particularly dependent upon the active involvement of each instructor and a continual flow of imaginative course proposals. A few of our instructors have not found the issues approach congenial and have had to take responsibility for the relative unpopularity of the surveys they insist on proposing. That instructors are unprotected by course requirements and must compete with colleagues for courses and students has threatened some teachers and produced occasional friction. On the whole, however, the faculty has responded positively to the opportunity to teach new materials from fresh points of view, and though we have not welcomed the extra work, we are aware that having constantly to restructure our courses makes us plan our work much more carefully than we might do otherwise. As a whole, we are happier than we were under the old curriculum.

James Bartell
Assistant Professor

Typical Courses Added in the Last Five Years
Major Principles in the Reading of Literature
Major Issues in English, American, Ancient, and Comparative Literature
Literature of Minority Groups
Topics in English, American, and Comparative Literature
Folklore
English Linguistics
English Grammar
Advanced Creative Writing
Readings in Medieval Literature
The Nature of Poetry
Literary Expressions of Underground Movements
Literature, Culture, and the Human Personality

Typical Courses Dropped in the Last Five Years
Literature as Experience
Biblical Backgrounds of Literature
Survey of English Literature
Survey of American Literature
The Essay
Greek Literature in Translation
History of the Drama
Modern English
Grammar for Teachers
Great Utopias (honors course)
Mythological Background of Literature
Roman Literature in Translation
Writing of Fiction
Enjoyment of Poetry
The Continental Novel

Most Popular Courses
Masterpieces of World Literature
Folklore
Shakespeare
Understanding Literature

Literary Expressions of Underground Movements
Technical Report Writing
Writing Poetry and Fiction
Major Issues in American Literature
Topics in American Literature

Least Popular Courses
Major Issues in English Literature
Advanced Composition
Topics in English Literature
Afro-American Literature
Modern Drama
Readings in Comparative Literature after 1500
Problems in the Reading and Presentation of Literature
Topics in Comparative Literature

Courses Most Attractive to Nonmajors
Technical Report Writing
Writing Poetry and Fiction
Major Issues in American Literature
Literature of Minority Groups
Folklore
Literary Expressions of Underground Movements
Literature, Culture, and the Human Personality

Courses Most Attractive to Majors
Writing Poetry and Fiction
Major Principles in the Reading of Literature
Major Issues in American Literature
Literature of Minority Groups
Form and Theory in the Writing of Poetry and Fiction
English Linguistics
Advanced Creative Writing
Myth and Folklore
Literature, Culture, and the Human Personality

Major Changes in Curriculum
(1) Course offerings featuring practical reading and writing skills have been strengthened;
(2) specific requirements for the major have been dropped.

13

Ohio State University

If any courses may be said to be "saving" the department's enrollment, they are the introductions to fiction, folklore, and the Bible.

Chairman John Gabel
Ohio State University
164 West 17th Avenue
Columbus 43210

Full-Time Faculty 81

Calendar Quarter

Type of School Public research university

Requirements for Major Forty hours, plus one five-hour course in critical writing. No comprehensive examination.

Our undergraduate curriculum is to a degree schizophrenic. We are oriented toward the traditional in advanced courses for majors, and we are somewhat more flexible in the group of introductory courses we offer to satisfy the need of an enormous student body for courses fulfilling a university humanities requirement. The curriculum has developed more in response to particular demands made at particular times than to a careful plan for change. Within the past dozen years we have had two extensive examinations of the curriculum, one resulting in major changes and the other resulting in no changes; these spasms of self-questioning aside, we change slowly, under great pressure.

At the introductory level we offer a wide variety of courses from which students may choose whatever will fit their schedules and their personalities. These courses are populated chiefly by nonmajors from every college of this megaversity, required, as they all are, to have a passing acquaintance with "Man's Humane Achievements." For the relatively few lower division students who retain an interest in the traditional, we offer a sequence in Masterpieces of British Literature, a course in Masterpieces of American Literature, and an introductory course in Shakespeare. We have long offered generic introductions to fiction, poetry, and drama, in decreasing order of popularity. The fiction introduction and the American masterpieces course continue to attract large numbers of students; we teach numerous sections of each course every quarter. Students seem drawn to these courses for good reasons, including their own realization that they have read and will continue to read fiction if they read anything "literary" and their desire to know something about their own cultural heritage. Their other reasons include a (mistaken) presumption that there are tricks to reading poetry or drama which one does not have to worry about in reading fiction and a combination of chauvinism and the desire for relevancy which assumes that only American writers can speak to American readers. For six years we have had a course in Afro-American Literature; highly popular when it was introduced, this course has attracted fewer students over the last two years, possibly because the Black Studies Department on this campus has been unusually successful in attracting students to its own courses.

Our most consistently popular course, over a period of more than sixty years, has been The English Bible. For a long time it was taught by a distinguished veteran professor whose charisma was thought to account for its wide appeal; since his retirement it has been taught by many different faculty members to an ever-increasing audience. Those who take it include Fundamentalists, Jesus freaks, Jews, Presbyterians, Methodists, Muslims, and (the large majority) ordinary nonreligious undergraduates; they take it despite its reputation as a difficult course in which to get a high grade; they seem to take it for all kinds of reasons or for no discernible reason at all. We do not pretend to understand its popularity, but we offer as many sections of it as we can staff, each quarter of the year.

More recently, there has been far more demand than can be met for our introductory course in folklore. When it was first offered two years ago, in a single section for 45 students, almost 200 students signed up. Since then, the number of sections has been increased sharply but the demand has increased even faster. Students at an urban university seem drawn to the course for several reasons: they want to be put in touch with what they feel (rightly or wrongly) is authentic in the American past, what comes from the people rather than from the literati; those with rural forebears want to have a stronger sense of their personal heritage, as do the second and third generation descendants of the numerous ethnic communities in Ohio cities. By offering to acquaint them with what is quaint and homely rather than designedly artistic, the course may flatter the students' sense of their own sophistication; by asking them to do collecting projects rather than to write papers or take examinations, the course gives them an experience which they feel is somehow more "real" than that offered in standard literature courses. For many years one of our distinguished older professors taught a course in folklore as an occasional sideline; we now employ two full-time folklorists, and two or three other faculty members regularly teach in the program. If any courses may be said to be "saving" the department's enrollment, they are the introductions to fiction, folklore, and the Bible.

In the past few years we have offered a variety of open-topic courses, one available only to freshmen, the others to upperclassmen. Most of these offerings have been one-shot affairs dealing with an aspect of popular culture or with a special literary phenomenon, including science fiction, mystery and detective fiction, the Indian in American literature, and the literature of sports. Two new courses, to be taught this year for the first time as part of our regular offerings, have grown out of the open-topic courses. One of these, Thematic Approaches to Literature, is intended to cross the boundaries of genre and historical period; since most of our students would much rather talk about themes than analyze techniques, we expect this course to draw well. The other, Women in Literature, has been offered several times to large and appreciative classes and should continue to do well.

We anticipate further additions to our introductory courses, probably in the form of new thematic studies; possibilities include science fiction, the literature of minority cultures, and literature and popular culture. We have had no regular course in this department in film and literature; but a number of our professors have experimented with film in established literature courses, and it is likely that film and literature will become a separate subject of study before long.

We believe that diversity is healthy for our faculty, since it encourages the development of a variety of interests, and is essential for our survival, since we must now actively compete for students. A combination of changes in the university (a drop of 16 hours in the total graduation requirement, a deliberate cut of almost 50 percent in the number of Education English majors, a liberalization of earlier university humanities requirements) and a relaxation in rules governing our own major has relieved students of the obligation to take certain of our courses; indeed, students other than literature majors can, if they work at it, avoid taking any literature courses at all. As a result, we are trying to become better at finding out what students want and more efficient at supplying what they want. Such "academic merchandising" is, of course, offensive at times to our faculty, but the unfortunate truth is that we are no longer in a sellers' market.

Our advanced courses, intended primarily for English majors and upper level students in other areas of the humanities, follow a much more traditional pattern. We offer separate courses on three major figures (Chaucer, Shakespeare, Milton) as well as historically divided courses in all periods from medieval to contemporary. In recent years we have dropped a requirement that all majors finish their program with a tutorial course culminating in a comprehensive examination. That change has relieved most majors of any pressure to try for broad coverage and has contributed to the diminished enrollment in most courses dealing with literature before 1800. Our heaviest enrollment has been, predictably, in American and contemporary literature, but we are now experiencing a drop in enrollment in all of our five courses in twentieth-century literature, a drop which may be temporary or may signal renewed interest in courses dealing with older literature. Total enrollment in the advanced courses has stabilized, and since the number of majors has been on the increase we expect enrollment to hold. The increase in the number of majors has been a surprise. It is not a sign of a new surge of interest in graduate study in English, however, but apparently the result of several developments: the publicity given to the desire of law schools for English majors, a new advising system for majors, and increased attention to the undergraduate program by the entire department.

Because few of our majors intend to go on to graduate school, we are pleased that our major is totally unstructured. Each student majoring in English must take at least five advanced courses, but any combination of five of our thirty-two undergraduate courses meets the formal requirement. The student is thus free to pursue his or her interest in a particular historical area or a particular genre or discipline and to shape a program suited to special talents rather than to a predetermined framework. If we are uncomfortable because we cannot certify that each of our majors "knows" certain things about literature, we can at least claim to have provided for our students the opportunity to choose from a variety of periods; because of the diversity of our faculty, students are inevitably exposed to a number of different ways of approaching the study of literature.

Two other aspects of our undergraduate curriculum deserve mention. We maintain a set of honors courses instituted eight years ago to permit especially talented students to undertake intensive studies in seminar situations. These students are encouraged to begin their programs with a proseminar in a single figure and to continue with one or two advanced honors seminars, which parallel our regular upper level offerings. Since it is from this small group of students that most of our applicants for graduate school come, we encourage them to seek a broader historical coverage than most of our regular majors trouble to obtain. Students in the honors program can graduate with distinction if they write an honors essay; about three a year choose to do so.

We also have a program in creative writing, which we have deliberately kept relatively small. We offer introductory and advanced courses in the writing of fiction and the writing of poetry. Four faculty members devote most of their time to these courses, and the courses are almost always full. Each year there are a few students who arrange their programs to get what amounts to a major in creative writing.

We have been slow to alter the structure of our courses at the advanced level; over the past six years, the only change of substance has been an increase from three to five in the number of courses offered in twentieth-century literature. The very diversity in academic attitudes among our faculty creates a tension which probably assures that we will not change radically unless faced with a catastrophic drop in the number of majors. We retain a strong and usually healthy respect for the conventional, but we will continue to be flexible and as innovative as possible in meeting the changing demands of the great mass of nonmajors who consume most of our teaching energies.

John M. Muste
Professor and Vice-Chairman

Courses Added in the Last Five Years
Thematic Approaches to Literature
Women in Literature
Introduction to Folklore
Introduction to English Language Study
Afro-American Language
Applied English Phonology
Milton
Twentieth-Century Poetry
Literature since 1945
Group Studies (freshman)
Group Studies (advanced)

Courses Dropped in the Last Five Years
Literary and Cultural Heritage of the Middle
    East

Most Popular Courses
Introduction to Folklore
Introduction to Fiction
The English Bible
Masterpieces of American Literature
Shakespeare

Least Popular Courses
Masterpieces of English Literature
The English Renaissance
Nineteenth-Century Prose
Restoration and Eighteenth-Century Drama

Major Changes in Curriculum
The comprehensive examination has been dropped; it has resulted in only students with plans for graduate school trying for historical coverage while the majority simply take what appeals to them, usually shying away from courses in periods before 1800.

14

Pfeiffer College

When our enrollment dropped to five to ten students per class, we had to compensate with excellent content and enthusiasm on the part of our teachers in order to try to build enrollment.

Chairman Nancy D. McLaurin
Pfeiffer College
Box T
Misenheimer, North Carolina 28109

Full-Time Faculty 6

Calendar Semester

Type of School Private liberal arts college

Requirements for Major 350 units (an "A" in a 3-hour course has the equivalent of 30 units; "B" through "F" on sliding scale) including genre, survey, two-semester sequence in the drama or the novel, Backgrounds to Literature, The Grammars of English, Shakespeare.

In 1968 the Pfeiffer College Department of English put into practice curriculum changes we had been working on since 1964. By faculty vote, it had been decided that each department offering a major should select all courses to be taken by students majoring in that subject; and it developed that few wanted their students to take freshman English—or any other English course. Therefore, since English majors had access to other composition courses, we dropped the two semesters of freshman composition and literature. Within three years, however, in response to faculty demand, we again scheduled composition. We constructed our "new" composition course to meet the basic needs of students in majors other than English. If an English major has to take the basic composition course, he gets credit toward graduation but *not* toward an English major.

At Pfeiffer College, each composition class has a maximum enrollment of 18 students, an "ideal" enrollment of 16. At the time we instituted this course, we knew of no other college or university that had one similar to it, though since then a number of schools have studied our program and adopted it or independently instituted a variation of it. Our composition classes meet for one one-hour session and for one two-hour session each week (a few sections now meet 1½ hours twice a week). During the one-hour segment, the instructor lectures, explains, or discusses material; during the two-hour segment, the instructor and student assistants, selected for their knowledge of, and ability to communicate, techniques in writing and grammatical structure, work in the classroom with the students. Each student assistant works in a tutorial capacity with about four composition students, giving them intensive guidance and help under the direction of the instructor. One of the three hours is used for theme writing, which is always done in the classroom. The teacher grades all papers and plans the tutorial study; the student assistants carry out the directives of the teacher, with the teacher moving from table to table to give further instructions or to answer questions. If a student needs more tutorial assistance in grammar or writing than class time permits, he is able to attend Writing Workshop to get extra help. In Writing Workshop, an instructor and student assistants give help on a one-to-one basis to any student who seeks it. This method of teaching composition allows the professor to cut student theme conferences to a minimum outside the actual class hours and to schedule more office time for *all* students who want conferences with the professor. This teamwork (student assistants working with professors) is succeeding better than any other method we have tried. Our failures, which used to be 30 to 40 percent each semester, now are only ten percent, excluding students who drop out. Fortunately, from the inception of this program, even though administrations at Pfeiffer College have changed, each has concurred in the belief that this is a total-college project worthy of support. Therefore, the student assistants are paid to work in a program that has the support of administration and faculty. Our teacher education program requires participation as a composition assistant on the part of each English major who is certifying to teach so that he can gain experience and confidence.

All compositions are written in class, but corrections and revisions may be constructed out of class. No composition is considered complete until the revision has been accepted and filed; the revision completes the assignment but does not change the grade. After the student writes six acceptable papers (grade C- or above) and passes a grammar examination, he, the professor, and his student assistant check his folder to ascertain that all materials are in it and are complete. If the check is positive, the student receives his final grade in the course and may leave the class unless he elects to remain and try to raise his grade. An "early release" is highly probable for the student who enters with a rather good high school background; in as short a time as eight weeks, this student can receive his final grade in the course. Because students are coming to us less and less well prepared in writing and knowledge of grammar, we do not expect all of them to complete the composition requirement in one semester. Therefore, we have an arrangement with the registrar's office and the Vice-President for Academic Affairs by which the student takes composition until he passes, whether the time be eight weeks or nine months.

Students who work hard and make progress but achieve less than the required amount by the end of the semester get a grade of "Incomplete." These students register again for the course, not necessarily under the same instructor, and continue their work until they complete the requirements. They do NOT begin over under the system. Because of the nature of the course, the student's file folder has his complete record and is available for any instructor to interpret. These students may finish the course in another three weeks or may need the rest of another semester.

When we dropped our two-semester freshman English course, we replaced three hours of it with Backgrounds to Literature, a study of archetypes and themes as they have appeared in literature and other areas from ancient to modern times. In Backgrounds, the student is introduced to such themes as the Hero, the Scapegoat, the Quest, the Dying God, etc., with literary examples ranging from myths of many lands, *Gilgamesh, Oedipus,* and *Beowulf* to Malamud, Eliot, and Golding. Realizing that we had too much in this course to include teaching the research paper, we instituted a one-hour research techniques course that meets for twelve hours prior to mid-term; the student is required to take this prior to or simultaneously with Backgrounds to Literature, the course in which he puts into practice the techniques he has learned in the research course. We now have an enrollment in Research Techniques of over 100 students each semester out of a total student body of 850 to 900. Backgrounds is an extremely demanding course but exciting to student and teacher. Each semester we close (at 25) every section we offer; if we had the instructional personnel, we could fill more sections. This course, one of our hardest on the freshman or sophomore level, has grown each year in popularity. Micro-courses (explained later), which have developed as a result of Backgrounds, have caused more students to want to take it. The first year we offered Backgrounds to Literature, however, we had disastrous results. Since no English was required and few elected it, enrollment in our classes was almost uniformly under ten, frequently five to eight. A good result of this enrollment was that it gave the professors time to work on course content and methodology: we *had* to make the courses interesting enough to lure more students. A potential problem remained in our high academic standards, which could easily deter students from electing English courses. In spite of this, we maintained standards and tried to make the courses sell themselves.

At the same time that we changed the freshman course, we dropped the two-semester English Literature Survey and instituted genre courses in poetry, fiction, and introduction to drama. We did this because former graduates who were teaching or were in graduate schools reported to us that the survey came too early in the program; those graduates who were teaching also complained they had to teach genres they had never really studied.

Because we needed to give a comprehensive picture of all of English literature at some place in the student's curriculum, we designed a one-semester-hour survey of English literature to be taken in the senior year when the student has completed most of his English major and is ready for an intensive survey that will bring together all that he has learned. We added a one-semester-hour American literature course to be taken by the student one of the last three semesters before he graduates. In this each student does an intensive study of one American writer; he gives an oral report on his subject every two weeks.

We had thought the result of dropping the sophomore survey would be poorer backgrounds for other courses. This has proved to be wrong (thank goodness). The material covered in Backgrounds, Poetry, Fiction, and Introduction to Drama has given the student more stability and reference points than we had thought possible. In addition, each English major is required to take a two-semester sequence in Development of Drama plus Contemporary Drama or the English Novel plus Modern Novel. These chronologically arranged courses provide the "survey reference points" the student needs.

In Backgrounds to Literature and in the genre courses, a basic part of the program is composition. In each of these, four to six short critical essays and a research paper are written, graded for composition as well as content, and returned to the student for revision. Because of our emphasis on written (and oral) communication, our literature courses are generally limited to twenty-five students. In our advanced courses we have smaller enrollments (12 to 17 in each) and as a result can, and usually do, require at least as much writing and oral participation as we do in the lower level courses.

Conferences with our graduates caused us to make other curriculum changes. We combined the Romantic and Victorian courses to form a one-semester Nineteenth Century survey which gives the student an excellent background for teaching or for pursuing these areas on a specialized level in graduate school. We added a course in the nondramatic literature of the Renaissance to complement the course in Shakespeare. With these additions, we had courses that covered most of English literature, and we could reasonably expect a major to graduate with few "gaps" in his background. There is no doubt that the professors miss our old two-semester English Literature Survey, but all agree that our new program is undoubtedly serving our students better than the old one did.

In addition to Backgrounds, Poetry, Fiction, and Introduction to Drama, English majors are required to take a course in the Grammars of English (part traditional, part transformational) and advanced work in writing (advanced composition, creative writing, or other writing). They must take a two-semester survey of American literature, one semester of Shakespeare, either Chaucer or Milton, and a two-semester sequence in the novel or the drama. Also, to satisfy half of a two-course (or one course plus honors) religion requirement, they take Literature of the Bible, taught by a professor of English.

Beyond these courses, majors can elect the remainder of their units from Southern Literature, the Renaissance, the Eighteenth Century, the Nineteenth Century, Modern Poetry, or World Literature (to the Renaissance). Each student majoring in English is required to take 350 units in this department but is not limited to that number.

The major and nonmajor alike have access to other literary areas via micro-courses which supplement the student's academic fare. Between five and ten years ago, Pfeiffer instituted a system by which the student earns up to 125 units (roughly equivalent to 5 3-semester-hour courses with a grade of "B"). Of the 125 "supplementary" units accepted for graduation, the student is required to have 30 in the area of Language and Literature (including Drama). Out of this has grown one of our greatest strengths as well as our most lamentable weakness.

The strength of this program lies in the micro-courses that have evolved. Any professor who wishes to give several lectures on a "pet" subject compiles a syllabus, including a reading list if he chooses, and submits it to the head of his department or division and to the chairman of the supplementary program. If the course is approved, it appears as a part of the registration materials for the next semester. The number of lectures for micro-courses has varied in this division from four to seven; the subjects are manifold. Among the micro-courses we have offered are the following:

> John Donne
> Beaumarchais
> Surrealism and Dadaism
> Old Southwestern Humor
> History of the English Language
> Cult and the Occult; grew out of the Backgrounds to Literature
> Black Poetry
> English Usage
> The Arthurian Legend (a 3-hour course has evolved from this micro-course)
>
> Eugene O'Neill
> Lillian Hellman
> Edward Albee
> Tennessee Williams
> Arthur Miller
> Archetypes in Children's Literature
> William Inge

The number of units that may be accumulated in each course varies from an automatic one half for each hour of attendance to one full unit for each hour depending on the amount of work the student does.

The greatest value of the micro-courses is that they stimulate interest in some of our regular three-hour courses. A student who elects a micro-course in Archetypes to Children's Literature, for instance, may well discover that the same archetypes are also discussed more extensively in Backgrounds to Literature; he may enroll in Contemporary Drama as a result of attending micro-courses in Eugene O'Neill or Arthur Miller; or the micro-course in Negro poetry may cause him to register for Modern Poetry in which the students study Black poetry for about one third of the course. One professor is even incorporating a micro-course into her regular semester course next spring in an effort to advertise what may be found in the genuine course and perhaps stimulate enrollment for the next class. In a liberal arts college of fewer than 1,000 students, this method gives an excellent opportunity to the teacher to lecture on a subject of his own interest even though he may not be able to offer a full course in it. At times it gives the student an opportunity to see in brief some of the ideas that may be discovered in the semester courses.

The weakness in our supplementary program, which is under study at present, is that in order to offer enough events to give the student flexibility in choosing programs for the required number of units, we have offered some TV programs or films that we found—too late—were worthless. We hope to remedy this situation very soon.

In order to boost enrollment in English classes, we instituted a major in English-Drama to provide the student with background enough in drama to go on to graduate school. We had no major in drama at that time; we still do not have one, but this combination major seems to be doing very well. If the student wishes to certify to teach, he must add more English courses and certify in that area.

In 1974 the faculty voted to start a comparative literature minor with courses being drawn from the areas of English, French, and German literature (all taught in English). We expect this new area to draw even more students.

A new major area we are now working on which has received Academic Council approval and, after a bit more work, will be submitted to the faculty, is one in humanities that will require seven or more courses to be taken in the Department of Language and Literature. We expect this to increase further enrollment in our English classes. The factor about this new major which we hope will lure more students is that we offer with it a "minor" area which will prepare the students for careers in business and industry rather than the usual teaching, etc.

At this time, enrollment in our courses seems to be increasing rather than decreasing. Part of this increase comes from the fact that once again most students are now required to take two or three English courses; they may find that they like them and register for more. When our enrollment dropped to five to ten students per class, we *had* to compensate with excellent content and enthusiasm on the part of our teachers in order to try to build enrollment. If I had to designate the element that has stimulated most this slow but certain gain in our English classes in recent years, it would be the trauma we experienced when we realized almost overnight that not only was the English major in jeopardy but so were our jobs. In order to retain both, we had to be creative while maintaining integrity in our academic standards. We had to convince faculty and students that English is a vital part of their education and lure the students to elect courses that demand hard work—reading, writing, and thinking. As a result we have some very creative teaching in the Department of Language and Literature. Our professors are encouraged to teach rather than write, to channel their energies into their classes, and their research into their teaching areas. All in all, things are far from perfect; but here at Pfeiffer the situation in English is improving each year—and, compared to five years ago, we are well off indeed.

Nancy D. McLaurin
Chairman

Courses Added in the Last Five Years
The Nineteenth Century
The Renaissance
Seminar in English Literature
Seminar in American Literature
Research Techniques

Courses Dropped in the Last Five Years
The Romantic Period
The Victorian Period
Literary History of England

Most Popular Courses
Backgrounds to Literature
Literature of the Bible

Development of the Drama
Contemporary Drama
The English Novel
The Modern (World) Novel
Southern Literature
Shakespeare
Chaucer
Modern Poetry

Least Popular Courses
Introduction to Drama
Survey of American Literature
Eighteenth Century
Advanced Composition

Courses Most Attractive to Nonmajors
Modern Novel
Development of Drama
Contemporary Drama

Shakespeare
Literature of the Bible
The Grammars of English
Modern Poetry

Major Changes in Curriculum
The curriculum has been extended to include a "tangential" major—English-Drama—with plans for such in comparative literature, business, and humanities.

15

Rollins College

Nearly half the classes currently offered by the English department are service courses.

Chairman Cary D. Ser
Rollins College
Winter Park, Florida 32789

Full-Time Faculty 9

Calendar 4-1-4

Type of School Private comprehensive college

Requirements for Major Twelve courses, including Medieval and Renaissance, Restoration, eighteenth and nineteenth centuries, Introduction to Literary Study, two courses in American literature, three courses in English literature before 1900, three electives in language and literature, and independent study. No comprehensive examination.

Ten years ago all undergraduate English majors at Rollins College were required to take a three-course survey of English literature from *Beowulf* through the Restoration, eighteenth-century poetry and prose, Romantic poets, Victorian poetry and prose or novel, two courses in Shakespeare, and a two-course survey of American literature; in addition, students were to elect a minimum of three courses in a specific field: the novel, the drama, creative writing, or twentieth-century literature. Since that time significant changes in the college curriculum have necessitated related alterations of the English major; moreover, the department itself has instituted refinements of its program in an effort to provide students with a solid background in English and American literature and an opportunity to specialize in areas of their individual interests.

When Rollins adopted a winter-term calendar in 1966, the freshman year was to be devoted to "foundation" courses in humanities, social sciences, and natural sciences, the sophomore and junior years to the completion of a major, and the senior year to interdisciplinary courses and seminars. This program failed for a number of reasons: first, few faculty members were prepared to teach interdisciplinary courses; second, students felt pressured to select and complete a major in two years; and third, there was no clear understanding of the relationship between the structure of the curriculum and the students' personal objectives. The English department committed three of its faculty to the humanities course, and these instructors were to "supervise" the composition skills of the entire freshman class. But when upperclassmen began to demonstrate an inability to write coherent papers and examinations, a traditional course in composition was reinstituted and was (and still is) required of all entering students who scored below 500 on the CEEB English Achievement Test. For a few years this course was widely despised.

In the meantime, the number of advanced literature and language courses offered by the department was significantly reduced. Although greater flexibility was introduced in the English undergraduate curriculum, students frequently complained that there was not enough time to complete the number of courses required for a major and that they did not have an opportunity to take as many English courses as they wished. Faculty members felt, moreover, that students preparing for graduate school were unable to acquire a broad literary background.

When the "foundation" program was scrapped two years ago, the curriculum began to assume a more traditional character. Although considerable experimentation continues during the short winter term, the longer fall and spring terms are given over to the offering of courses similar to those that were available at most colleges and universities in the 1950's. Freshmen now elect introductory courses to fulfill distribution requirements in humanities, social sciences, and natural sciences; and upperclassmen spend three years satisfying major requirements and sampling courses in areas of their choice. Surprisingly, most Rollins students seem to be quite happy with this arrangement. It is likely that their preoccupation with the current job market has led them to the conviction that an accumulation of courses within a narrow spectrum will enhance their chances of surviving in the "real" world.

Nearly half the classes currently offered by the English department are service courses: basic composition, introduction to literature, and expository writing. This has been necessitated not by a dramatic decline in the number of English majors, but by increasing demands from freshmen and nonmajors. Students who are required to take the composition course do so willingly; and many of those who are exempted actually feel cheated and fight for the rare vacancies that occur. The introduction to literature courses offered to fulfill humanities distribution requirements are extremely popular, and there is evidence that they are helping to attract majors. Enrollments in the expository writing courses are rapidly increasing: majors and nonmajors elect this course to improve their communications skills, and in recent years special sections—such as "expository writing for science majors"—have been created to accommodate specific student interests.

The English major now reflects a compromise between tradition and innovation, requirements and electives. All majors are required to take the two courses in major English writings (Medieval and Renaissance; Restoration, eighteenth and nineteenth centuries), introduction to literary study, any three courses in English literature before 1900, any two courses in American literature, any three electives in language and literature, and an independent study project. The introduction to literary study is designed to acquaint sophomores with the principal critical approaches to literature and with the major concepts, methods, and research tools essential to the study of literature; ideally, it should also provide our majors with a knowledge of the career opportunities available to them. The reading material in this course has been keyed to the readings assigned in the major writings courses, so that the works studied in the one class may be submitted to a variety of critical approaches. Our English majors seem to be happy with the curriculum: those few who are planning to earn advanced degrees are able to elect courses required or recommended for admission to graduate programs; those many who consider the B.A. as their terminal degree are able to elect courses in support of their interests.

The principal strength of our undergraduate curriculum is its service to a broad range of students. Nearly half our offerings each term are courses that satisfy the composition and humanities distribution requirements. These courses are always among the first to fill up during registration. While some members of the department would prefer to offer more courses for English majors every year, instead of in alternate years, it is generally agreed that our value to the college as a whole would thereby be diminished. Some of our majors are unhappy that a greater number of advanced language and literature courses cannot be offered each term, but they have had no difficulty in satisfying the requirements for the major. If there is a weakness in the curriculum, it would appear to be our inability to generate enthusiasm among majors for courses—such as literary criticism—that students planning to attend graduate school would normally elect; but then, graduate study does not seem to be a very attractive option for many of our students these days.

Last year our departmental faculty was reduced from ten to nine full-time members. Because the college has decided to reduce the faculty by fifteen percent during the next few years, it is likely that we will lose an additional instructor in the near future. In light of this paring and in light of the current trend among students to select career programs in nonhumanities areas, the current balance in our offerings of service and major courses would seem to be appropriate.

Edward H. Cohen
Associate Professor

Courses Added in the Last Five Years
Introduction to Literary Study
Selected Studies in Film
Selected Studies in Minority Literature
Expository Writing
Milton
Chaucer

Courses Dropped in the Last Five Years
Types of Literature

Most Popular Courses
Introduction to Literature
Selected Studies in Film
Selected Studies in Minority Literature
Expository Writing
Shakespeare
Twentieth-Century Drama
Twentieth-Century English Novel
Twentieth-Century British and American
    Poetry
Twentieth-Century American Novel

Least Popular Courses
Milton
Chaucer
Victorian Poetry and Essay
Literary Criticism

Courses Most Attractive to Nonmajors
Creative Writing
Themes in World Literature
Selected Studies in Film
Selected Studies in Minority Literature
Expository Writing
The English Language

Courses Most Attractive to Majors
American Literature
Shakespeare
Romantic Period
English Novel

Major Changes in Curriculum
(1) Nearly half the classes taught each term by the department are now service courses; (2) majors, who five years ago had only one elective available in their program, are now afforded greater flexibility in their choice of courses.

16

University of San Francisco

And whatever success our reforms had with the students who remain in the program, there is no denying that the English major itself has suffered a great loss of students.

Chairman Edward Stackpoole
University of San Francisco
San Francisco, California 94117

Full-Time Faculty 12

Calendar Semester

Type of School Private comprehensive university

Requirements for Major Thirty-six hours, including three courses in English literature prior to 1800.

The Courses

The department's offerings have been traditionally arranged according to period, genre, and author, and for the majority of the faculty, that remains the principal guide to course offerings. However, recent interest in linguistics, in national literatures besides English and American, and in comparative literature has brought thematic and topical courses into the catalog, and departmental hiring has to some extent reflected this broadening of interest. These additions come from a variety of motives. Linguistics has special importance in California for prospective teachers, as the state requires certain competencies in the field for both primary and secondary teachers; national literatures, from Korea, Japan, and Ireland, to name a few, reflect the interests of the university's high proportion of foreign-born students and the cosmopolitan expectations of the city of San Francisco. Comparative literature was chosen by the department as an area that might help attract new students to the major, or at least to several courses. We have also added a number of courses in Black literature, both American and African, in the past five or six years, and these are provided through cooperation with the university's ethnic studies department.

The Curriculum

English majors are required to complete thirty-six units of English course work, nine of which must come from periods before 1800. Otherwise, there are no departmental requirements. This curriculum was adopted about five years ago, when the university Academic Vice-President eliminated many university-wide requirements and made each department responsible for almost the entire curriculum of its majors. Some departments continued to require many courses outside their own fields, but the English department did not. Faculty and students met in an open forum and established two principles: first, students would have major responsibility for choosing a sequence of courses that would accommodate their own particular interests and needs; second, it was assumed that for a majority of students, a broad and unspecialized sequence of study would be preferred, and the department obliged itself to offer courses in a four-year cycle that would serve this purpose. To facilitate this, virtually all courses are offered without prerequisites.

The reform of the curriculum was frankly experimental. The most frequent and most vociferous complaint heard in those days was directed against required courses. They were felt to be drudge work, by both faculty and students, and the problem of motivation for work that was undertaken to "fulfill requirements" seemed overwhelming. There is no longer the violent antiestablishment rhetoric of those days, but the change was not a panacea, and we now hear that students want more "system," more "direction." And whatever success our reforms had with the students who remain in the program, there is no denying that the English major itself has suffered a great loss of students.

Further adjustment of the curriculum is certainly ahead. Two years ago, a novel M.A. exam system was initiated, and this year the freshman English offerings were changed in significant ways. The M.A. exam previously had been a traditional summary test, covering all of the major areas of English literature, and either passing or failing the student on the way to a degree. In order to minimize the summary aspects of the exam, we changed it into a course, Reading for Examination, which is based on an approved reading list composed by the student and an examining committee. The student is examined orally at the end of the semester, and the results are graded on the standard A-F scale. This grade takes its part in the student's overall grade point average, and if a student has been only marginally successful in course work, a failed exam can mean a failed program. But for most, the exam is an academic experience which does not threaten their entire program, and it is for the faculty a final view of the student's ability to cope with academic peers in a dynamic situation and can be recalled for use in letters of recommendation.

The new freshman course offerings began by dividing what had come to be a doubled topic. Our freshman courses were named by genre, and were at once an introduction to literature and a freshman composition course. Teachers found that student motivation was confused. Some were bored by composition and paid attention to only the literary aspects of the course. Others had little interest in literature, were taking the course as a requirement for some other department, and resented obligations to learn "criticism." We now offer two courses, one a composition series, taught to classes, maximum size fifteen. Another series comprises introductions to literature and is meant to serve both freshman and upper division nonmajor students. These courses are extremely varied and can be organized by theme, author, period, genre, methodology—indeed, anything the faculty member chooses. It is expected that a fair amount of experimentation and course-trying will go on in this series. One special feature of the composition course is that any student who does consistent honor work in the first weeks may, on the authority of the teacher, be assigned to a private reading program, which will be tutored by the instructor. This feature, of course, required the support of the university to the extent of limiting class size absolutely to fifteen.

Most Popular

Novel courses lead the way in popularity, no matter what period or country they focus on. After them, one can generalize that courses in modern literature are preferred over others. For a while, a course in film was very popular with nonmajors, but it is closer to other courses in size now as other film courses have become available through various departments. Shakespeare, Chaucer, and modern poetry are consistently popular.

New Directions

It is likely that in the future the department will emphasize the value of English as a preprofessional major. The university offers students the option of a double major, and there is some interest in developing a sequence in English that would suit students choosing this option. Extended offerings in writing, journalism, and interdisciplinary studies will probably be useful here. The value of reading courses that would appeal to nonmajors and maintain a high standard of academic activity is conceded by all, but so far no practical resolutions have been made toward this end.

Patrick Smith
Associate Professor of English

Courses Added in the Last Five Years
Writing i and ii
Introduction to Journalism
Advanced Studies in Journalism
Victorian Poetry and Prose
Western Voice in American Literature
Survey of Black Literature
American Criticism and Culture
Design of Language
Aspects of Language
Structuralism
Communication Systems
Modern Grammar
Linguistics for Credential Candidates
Modern Short Story
European Romantic Movement
Reading Literature
Creating the Literary History of
    San Francisco
Analysis and Expression of the Experience of
    Literature

Harlem Renaissance Writers
Introduction to Japanese and Korean
    Literature
Introduction to Chinese Literature
Elements of Film
Psychology and Literature

Courses Dropped in the Last Five Years
Modern Composition
Studies in Fiction (Drama, Poetry, Essay)

Least Popular Courses
Victorian period courses
Linguistics
Eighteenth Century

Most Popular Courses
Criticism and Film
Novel courses, any country, mostly modern
Shakespeare
Chaucer

17

San Francisco State University

The primary objectives are to teach what we are a department of in a form that says something to the generation of students sitting in front of us.

Chairman Graham Wilson
San Francisco State University
1600 Holloway Avenue
San Francisco, California 94132

Full-Time Faculty 68

Calendar Semester

Type of School Public comprehensive university

Requirements for Major Pattern A: one course in Shakespeare; one each in a literary period, genre, and individual author; one course in criticism or theory; one course in language; seven additional courses (39 units total). Pattern B: one course in Shakespeare; one course in language; four courses in individual authors (authors must represent 3 genres); seven additional courses (39 units total). Pattern C: requirements decided by student (39 units total). Other requirements for Secondary Credential English Major. No comprehensive examination.

General Statement

Our primary objectives are to teach what we are a department of in a form that says something to the generation of students sitting in front of us, and, given the upper division dominance in the university today, a generation means about two and a half years.

This point is worth at least half-hearted pursuit. Since Galileo, astronomy courses have seldom featured Copernicus. A twenty-year-old biology text is practically useless in the classroom today. Everyone knows and accepts this, but everyone thinks that the structure of English remains much the same, except that writers keep adding a story or two. However, a twenty-year-old linguistics text or survey of literature text is almost useless, for time not only adds to but changes our past. English language and literature have lately acquired Blacks, social dialects, women, psycholinguistics, language acquisition myths, radicals, homosexuality, about 400 Equal Opportunity Program students in writing a semester, and film. As a result of these "acquisitions" the department has developed appropriate courses that reflect the interests of these groups. (See Pilot Project.)

We haven't done as much about our suddenly modified inheritance as perhaps we could have, but we monitor both the real and the academic worlds with a committee setup worthy of Congress. William Harvey published his discovery of the circulation of the blood in 1628; in 1799 someone bled George Washington to death. This is quite a cultural lag. We in English have dramatically abridged all this. Someone "discovered" Blacks about ten years ago, and the next day we were teaching social dialects.

All this concerns the "what" of the objectives. We also work on the "how." For some time now our Pilot Project has explored new kinds of learning—variable units, combinations of small groups and large groups in a single course (differentiated from the classical section meeting because, in our arrangement, the same instructor does it all; this is the result of financial exigency rather than pedagogical purity, but, nonetheless, it is exploratory), forays into the community for subject matter and examples, self-initiated projects, and so on.

These objectives are both behavioral and vocational, of course, but if our success were to be measured by the number of the undergraduate majors we feed into jobs for which we have specifically prepared them, we would have to confess to an occasional failure, except that decent humane education may contribute to the maintenance of sanity in an insane world. In point of fact, our majors go to law school, into elementary school teaching, on to credentials for high school or community college teaching, a variety of teaching programs, graduate schools, and armed services.

It is sometimes conceded by other educational institutions and universally acknowledged by our own English faculty that what is unique about the San Francisco State University English department is the people who teach our courses. There is probably something to this, considering the climate, the location, and the quarter of a century the recently retired chairperson devoted to staffing this department with teachers who are both competent and eager. This is quite a trick, since in English, as, say, in police work, the presence of one quality sometimes dampens the other.

Curriculum

The undergraduate curriculum is in a constant state of revision. The Pilot Project which now occupies almost twenty percent of our staff has within the last year been geared into our regular requirements. Also within the last year we have made curricular adjustments to handle the new General Studies program for an elementary credential, and made arrangements with speech, drama, and humanities to open the English umbrella over their majors, as required by the Ryan Act.

No date can be named as the one when major revision took place, but over the last six years we have increased the number of electives an English major may take and considerably reduced the traditional historical emphasis.

Graham Wilson
Chairman

Pilot Project

An experimental program at San Francisco State, the Pilot Project works with variations of unit assignments, combinations of small groups and large groups in a single course, nonclassroom hours to be arranged with instructor, self-initiated projects, and specialized subject matter. Following is a list of the Pilot Project courses offered in the fall of 1973 together with a sampling of faculty evaluations:

Hero and Anti-Hero	5 units	Incest: Implications of an Archetype	3 units
The American Jewish Writer	5 units	Science Fiction and Fantasy	4 units
Woman as Hero	6 units	Literature for the Adolescent	4 units
Literature and Psychology	5 units	Introduction to Lyric Poetry	1 unit
Arthurian Romance	5 units	Genius in *Moby-Dick*	1 unit
Literature/Psychology: Shakespeare	6 units	*Dubliners*	1 unit
Rise of Novel/Novelist	6 units	Creative Collaboration	2 units
American Literature—Twentieth Century	5 units	Sounds of Language	1 unit
Homosexual and Bisexual in Contemporary Literature	5 units	Grammars of Language	1 unit
Modern British Literature	5 units	English as Second Dialect and Reading Techniques	5 units
Anderson-Faulkner: Southern Novelists	4 units	Shakespeare Seminar: Forms of Drama	4 units
Hemingway	5 units	James Joyce	5 units
		ProSem: Survey English Literature	5 units

Hero and Anti-Hero

I've been astonished at the quantity and quality of the reading and writing of many students. The goof-offs will perform inadequately everywhere. . . . I have found being asked to conceive new courses, or old courses in new formats, very useful. . . . I think harder about what I'm doing. I see more clearly where I'm stuck in the mud as a teacher, and I'm stimulated to do a good job.

The American Jewish Writer

I especially enjoyed probing single texts in depth, an activity the three-unit course format ordinarily does not comfortably accommodate. . . . Although a number of students regularly showed up for office conferences, not nearly enough did so, even though I was available in my office at least five hours a week. Nor did these same missing students respond to my repeated invitations to come to my home for evening study sessions.

Woman as Hero

This semester I split the class into four small groups which met regularly for the second half of every time block. Each group had its own meeting place and its own group leader, a student from one of last year's 303 courses who wanted to go over the material again and was willing (and able) to be responsible for running group discussions. I rotated among the groups, knew in general what each would be discussing even when I wasn't there, and met biweekly with the group leaders to discuss how their groups were going, academic or personality problems they were having, and so forth. Before the course began, I had consulted with them frequently on how we should run the groups—how to choose them, how the group leaders should present themselves, what the limits of their responsibilities were—and on the order of books and assignments; I met with them at the end of the course to assess the whole experiment and suggest changes for next semester. Finally, the leaders wrote evaluations of their group experience.... The small groups saved me a certain amount of energy in that I wasn't responsible for running a full six hours of lecture-discussion a week; but I put extra time into supervising the group leaders, and of course I was always with students during all six weekly contact hours.

The small groups were clearly a success. The students in their questionnaires and the group leaders in their evaluations were almost unanimous in praising the experience. Group discussions tended to be a mixture of textual study and personal application, which was certainly my original intention. I often lectured in large group, and kept whatever discussion we had there focused on the books themselves.

Arthurian Romance

The additional units provided us with sufficient time to spend approximately two weeks on each work. In the three-unit course I never felt that I had been able to cover the reading adequately; the five-unit course did not leave me with this feeling. Each work was covered rather thoroughly to my satisfaction and, I hope, to the students'.

The class was divided into four groups of approximately five students each at the beginning of the semester. On either Tuesday or Thursday of each week I would meet with each group for a half hour. Thus, a typical class session would involve the following:

2:10-3:15, full class lecture-discussion; 3:15-3:30, break; 3:30-4:00, small group; 4:00-4:30, small group. However, as the class gradually became a learning community, the advantages of a small group were no longer needed. The entire class was able to enter into discussion freely and willingly. Meeting with small groups at the beginning of the semester seems to contribute toward a cohesive large class. Students were able to present their essays in the small groups (and in the full class) with success. Student comments on the essays were considered beneficial by other students. A three-unit course would not have provided the time for class presentation of essays.

I should mention that I did not use TBA [to be arranged] hours. We met twice a week from 2:10 to 4:30. Trying to coordinate my schedule and the students' schedules in order to arrange mutually acceptable TBA hours has always seemed to me too difficult to arrange. I much prefer five hours per week being set aside by the student at registration for the course.

Rise of Novel/Novelist

This experiment supplied both successes and failures.... The additional three hours of TBA, devoted to independent study on a tutorial basis, gave me a better than usual opportunity to work closely and more professionally with each student bent upon a special project.... I will speculate further. Unless I delude myself, overriding the idealistic and qualitative attractions of a six-unit course are the quantitative if more practical advantages, for faculty as well as for students. Specifically, the total intimidation of work pressures in *all* our courses weakened the commitment of both me and my students in English 314. Swamped by papers from and preparations for the eighty students in my two other courses, I could not and did not make this experimental course as stimulating as it should have been. Swamped by their own immersion in 15 to 18 units of work, my English 314 students could not and did not help me to make the course more stimulating.

Problems in American Identity

The fourth unit made it possible, with no sacrifice to the course's intellectual content, to create a sense of community and a highly reinforcing environment for all kinds of literary and personal exploration. Once again the course became a source of energy release for students, not an energy drain. And once again I'll stay by my vow from last semester never to consider teaching this course for three units again.

The Homosexual and Bisexual in Contemporary Literature

Some advantages of making the course five units:

1. I increased the reading list from seven to eleven books. I was able to require several books no longer "in print" in paperback editions.

2. I not only assigned three short papers on the literature, but I assigned a short story. When students were willing, we read them in class. Students also read their own poetry, and there was still time for a more personal paper.

3. Not being limited to fifty-minute discussions.

4. A chance to have some guest speakers and to allow student presentations about local events.

5. The freedom to talk about anything related to the course's themes since there was *also* enough time to talk about the literature.

6. Time occasionally to break up into small groups.

As in my other Pilot Project courses, it was a distinctly richer educational experience. The extra units allow us the luxury of regarding education as something more than the teaching of a certain content in a certain discipline. In answer to other faculty reservations about four-, five-, and six-unit courses, I can't honestly say whether students did 5/3's the work, although I tried to get them to do it. What I can say is that San Francisco State University gave its students a chance to have a personal and unusual experience in the classroom and the students took advantage of it.

Dickens

I will never teach Dickens again unless it is for six units. . . . The reason such high morale is possible is that the Pilot Project assures us that we *do* have the freedom and power to change and reshape our courses.

Studies in Modern British Literature

It was a good idea but not successful as a course. It was too ambitious and more suited to a graduate seminar than to an upper division course without any prerequisites. The course had its enthusiasts—about three of them, who liked its openendedness and its eclecticism. The rest were baffled and found themselves stopped before they even got to the heart of the course. It proved for me to be a rich and stimulating experience, so that as an exercise in self-improvement I would rate it very high. I don't think I will teach its likes again.

Hemingway

Our great problem initially was finding meeting places for the seminars. Unfortunately, my new office is too small, and we were forced to use and borrow available space in other offices, in the Library, and wherever. I dislike intensely this gypsy necessity, having to vagabond around campus, meeting in alleyways with students perched on radiators and whatever for lack of adequate space. Surely something should be done to relieve this situation.

Science Fiction and Fantasy

Although I had taught this particular course several times previously for three units, I wanted to teach it for four units for the following reasons: (1) more intensive examination of the novels; (2) additional time for small group discussion (classes in the past had been very large), and the presentation and discussion of science fiction films; and (3) study of additional novels.

There were, however, several problems which should be mentioned. First, many students sign up for this class because they think that it will be another wow-pop-groovy course in which they will learn little but be entertained much. When they discover, however, that they will have to read closely, write well, and discuss intelligently the novels under examination, the interest of some diminishes seriously. I am not sure, however, that I could teach the course other than as a substantial, regular literature course. But this is my problem.

Introduction to Lyric Poetry

The "experiment" in English 361 was to see whether a one-unit "Introduction to Lyric Poetry," meeting for the first six Wednesdays of the semester, from 7:00 to 9:45 p.m., would enable relatively unsophisticated students to discuss poetry meaningfully.

I was pleased to see that the enrollment for English 361 was good and that nonmajors were represented along with majors. After the first two hours, devoted to "how" a poem "means," we studied representative poems by Keats, Hopkins, and Yeats, through a combination of lecture and class discussion. I think that the one-unit designation was responsible—at least in part—for the liveliness and intensity of our discussion. The fact that the course was going to end after only six weeks caused many students to devote themselves immediately and wholeheartedly to English 361, making higher than usual demands on themselves, the material, and me. I think the one unit of credit generated an air of experimental openness, spontaneity, and adventurousness in the students—qualities absolutely crucial to any "introduction" to lyric poetry. The critical essays and my informal conversations with the class at a party which I gave at the end of the course convinced me that English 361 was an intellectual, pedagogical, and spiritual "success."

Dubliners

Once again, I feel, and the response of my students indicates that they feel, that this one-unit course in *Dubliners* is exactly trimmed to our needs. . . . I discover again what I learned when I last offered this same course, that the disadvantage of meeting one hour a week is largely in preventing the familiarity that is created when students meet frequently together. Yet I would argue strongly that this particular class be taught in exactly these hours, while I would think it generally a mistake to teach a single whole work on the one-hour-a-week basis. Allowing a week to lapse between discussions that are essentially discussions of the same thing only creates frustration and irritation. *Dubliners*, however, allows us to confront a complete and self-sufficient work each meeting, moving on to a new set of problems—however interrelated and similar—the following week. Therefore, I strongly suggest that one-unit courses focused on a collection of short stories, or on works that are essentially composites—perhaps Idylls of the King—be permitted the one meeting a week possibility, and I would feel it would be wiser to offer one-unit courses on a single totally integrated work—whether it be *Hamlet, Herzog,* or *Howards End*—in classes that meet more frequently.

The Grammars of Language

Despite the fact that I was overly ambitious in planning for this one-unit course given the second five weeks of the fall semester 1973 and consider the experiment something of a disaster, all but two of the students who took the course indicated that the learning experience had been a valuable one. . . . In terms of time spent on preparation and energy expended, this course was a nightmare for me. I am not sorry that I did it, but I would never willingly do it again. Since the students seem to be so enthusiastic about one-unit courses, however, I would consider doing a series on such topics as "The English Verb Systems," "English Modal Auxiliaries," "English Articles and Pre-Articles," "English Clause Structure," and so on. With chunks of subject matter like this it should be possible for students, in five weeks, to cover the material in some depth and relate their findings to the teaching of composition and English grammatical structure in English as a second language. . . . In short, a one-unit course of clearly defined, if somewhat modest, proportions should be more satisfying for both the students and the teacher.

Most Popular Courses
Tutoring in Reading
Science Fiction and Fantasy
Women in Literature: Authors and
   Characters
Modern Fiction (both British and American)
Shakespeare: Rep. Plays/Selected Plays
Contemporary Literature
Romantic Movement
Short Story
Various Selected Studies (interdisciplinary
   studies, current interest areas)
Individual Authors (esp. American and/or
   novelists)

Least Popular Courses
Today's students are *today* oriented. Generally speaking they do not voluntarily take courses in the earlier periods, though they appreciate some of them when they do. Old English will not fill with the best instructor in the department, but just anyone can draw a roomful for a well-known contemporary author.

18

Virginia Commonwealth University

The weakness in our curriculum is that we still do not know enough about how to adapt ourselves or, for that matter, what to adapt to; its strength is that we have learned and adapted as much as we have.

Chairman Thomas Inge
Virginia Commonwealth University
901 West Franklin Street
Richmond 23220

Full-Time Faculty 46

Calendar· Semester

Type of School Public doctoral-granting university

Requirements for Major Twelve hours, including six hours from each of the following areas: English Literature; American Literature; Comparative Literature; Linguistics, Criticism, and Advanced Writing. No comprehensive examination.

Virginia Commonwealth University is a new urban university located in Richmond, Virginia; it was formed in 1968 by the merger of Richmond Professional Institute and the Medical College of Virginia. During the past five years the university has changed significantly: its practical purpose has been more clearly defined—to meet the needs of Richmond and the surrounding area. The nature of the student body has changed—over ten percent of the students are now Black. And the quality of its faculty has been improved. Five years ago, for example, 14 full-time members of the English department held Ph.D.'s; today, 28 full-time faculty hold the degree. The development of the freshman, sophomore, and upper division programs in English reflects these changes in purpose, student body, and faculty.

English 101-102, Freshman Composition and Rhetoric, is required by all undergraduate degree programs in the university. Thus, the freshman program is the largest in the department, enrolling over 1,700 students this fall. To meet the needs and interests of a diverse student body, we have changed the program considerably in the last five years. Until the fall of 1971, we taught a traditional composition course (multitheme reader plus *Harbrace Handbook*) during the first semester and an introduction to the genres of literature during the second. Attempting to make the content of the first semester more stimulating to students, we shifted to a thematic approach in the fall of 1971, allowing students and instructors to choose from a variety of seven thematic courses. At the same time, in an effort to change the second semester into a real service course, we shifted its emphasis from introducing students to literature to teaching them to write about techniques and themes in literature, requiring the same number of papers in the second semester as in the first. Students liked being able to choose from a number of different themes for 101, but a number of faculty felt that teaching a theme interfered with the teaching of basic writing skills. The same problem existed in 102: we could not teach literature and writing to our students at the same time.

In 1973-74, we reexamined the whole freshman program, sending questionnaires to all department chairmen in the university in an attempt to determine the needs of students and our effectiveness in meeting these needs. The assistant dean of each school met with our faculty to discuss results of the questionnaires. After these discussions, we realized that we still were not training students adequately in the fundamentals of effective writing or preparing them to write the longer research papers they would be assigned in other courses. For 1974-75, we again revised the program: the title of the course was changed from Composition and Literature to Composition and Rhetoric; more important, we eliminated the thematic approach from 101 and the literature from 102. During the first semester, we teach basic writing and simple reading skills; during the second, we emphasize critical thinking, analysis of evidence and research techniques, and persuasion and style. Thus, the purpose of the whole freshman program is to make students more effective writers and intelligent readers. Judging by national trends and responses of faculty from other departments within the university, if we had not made freshman English a uniform two-semester writing course, some departments would probably have abolished their two-semester requirement.

Until 1970-71, there was little provision in the freshman program for either the outstanding or the weak student. A one-semester honors course had been tried but discontinued, and Review of English Fundamentals, a noncredit remedial course, had been dropped because the department could not receive full-time employee credit for teaching noncredit courses. Since 1970-71, no honors program has been established, but a number of students are now exempted from and given credit for one or both semesters through CLEP or Advanced Placement. Students may receive CLEP credit for 101 through the CLEP general examination or the subject examination; they may also receive credit for 102 through the subject examination. For the fall of 1974, seven of the Advanced Placement students who entered the university received credit for 101 and one for both 101 and 102. In addition, for the past two years, approximately four percent of the entering freshmen have been exempted from and given credit for 101 on the basis of the departmental placement examination. For the future, we plan to study the CLEP examination, especially the general examination, to see whether it is an adequate measure of a student's writing skills. We also plan to discover whether more students should be allowed exemption-credit for the first semester and whether we can extend exemption-credit to the second.

The number of students at Virginia Commonwealth whose writing skills are weak has increased dramatically in the past few years. A number of these students enter the university through a federally funded Special Services Program. Each summer, the department provides a bridge-the-gap noncredit course in elementary writing skills for this program. During the regular academic year, we teach special composition and rhetoric courses for all students whose writing skills are weak. These special classes grant the same credit as the regular composition and rhetoric classes, but they meet four times per week instead of the usual three, and their enrollment is limited to fifteen students per section. Instructors of these classes are members of our regular faculty who volunteer to teach them; they meet frequently to discuss problems and exchange ideas. A majority of the students in these classes complete them with a grade of C or better. However, because too many are not able to complete 101 or 102 successfully within a single semester (for the fall of 1973, 24 percent withdrew or failed and 15 percent received D's), we plan to begin using a "PR" grade. Students who are making satisfactory progress but who have not learned all the necessary skills taught in either semester will receive a "PR" at the end of the semester. During the next semester, they will be enrolled in special laboratory sections. We are also considering establishing a two-credit preparatory course for some of these students or perhaps shifting the whole program to a laboratory setting.

Our sophomore program consists of six survey courses in Western World Literature, English Literature, and American Literature. Since these are not continuous courses, students fulfilling a two-semester English elective requirement or a humanities requirement may take any of the six. Because a number of schools in the university have dropped the specific requirement of sophomore English and because students may now take upper division courses without fulfilling a sophomore prerequisite, enrollment in all the sophomore courses has decreased sharply, from approximately 1,600 students in the fall of 1970 to approximately 1,100 students in the fall of 1974, a drop of over 30 percent. But while enrollment in both the world and English surveys has been decreasing, that in the American surveys, which were shifted from the junior to the sophomore level in the spring of 1971, has risen from 54 students in the fall of 1971 to 273 students in the fall of 1974. The American literature surveys are popular because students consider American literature more immediate and relevant than world or English literature and because some of the department's most popular teachers are in this area. This rise in enrollment in the American surveys represents the equivalent of two faculty positions.

Presently, the Departmental Sophomore Committee is reconsidering the whole sophomore program. In the late spring of 1974, a new course, Topics in Language or Literature, described in the *VCU Bulletin* as "an in-depth study of a selected topic or genre in language or literature, or study of any non-western literatures," was added to the curriculum. We hope that as topics of interest to the students are taught under this number, enrollment in the sophomore program will increase. We are also experimenting with some interdisciplinary offerings on the sophomore level by scheduling surveys back-to-back with courses in art history and American history. For the past two years, a world literature course has been scheduled with an art history course, and this fall a first semester American literature course was scheduled with an American history course. Although enrollments have been small in these sections (usually about half of the enrollment of an ordinary survey), students who take these courses enjoy them. When students in the courses were asked why they thought more students had not enrolled, most replied that the courses had not been publicized enough.

At present, the department has forty-eight courses on the junior-senior level. These courses offer a broad range of choice for the student: figure courses; period courses; courses that combine a genre and period such as Modern Novel, Modern Poetry, Modern Drama, or Medieval Epic and Romance; linguistics courses; creative writing courses; courses in comparative literature and criticism; and junior and senior seminars. In addition, there are two courses in Black literature (Black American Writers and African Literature, both cross-listed with the Afro-American Studies Program), a course in the Bible as Literature, cross-listed with the Department of Philosophy and Religious Studies, a course in Minority Voice in American Literature, and a course titled Fiction into Film.

An examination of the courses added in the past five years (24 courses, almost half of our current offerings) reveals how much the upper division curriculum has changed. These changes came in three waves, each a response to particular circumstances. Nine courses were added for the year 1969-70; most of these are fairly standard undergraduate courses, added to close gaps in the department's offerings for majors. Two of these courses, English Literature, 1890-1918, and Medieval Epic and Romance, not so standard for an undergraduate curriculum, were added because of the interests of particular faculty members. English Literature, 1890-1918, has been offered only once since its inception, because the instructor who taught it is no longer with the department; Medieval Epic and Romance, on the other hand, has been offered a number of times and is particularly popular with students, primarily because of the reputation of the instructor who teaches it. The senior seminar was also added for 1969-70, and has usually attracted students, depending on the topics offered. These topics have ranged widely: Old English, Myth and Literature, Hawthorne and Melville, Faulkner, etc. The Faulkner seminars, offered twice, have been especially popular with students. For 1971-72, we added the junior seminars; this fall, both the seminar in Form and Theory of Poetry and the Gothic Spirit in Literature are filled to their maximum of fifteen students.

In 1970-71, the second wave of course additions was put into effect. The one course in the English novel was split into two, eighteenth and nineteenth centuries. But the major additions were in the American literature offerings: the six members of the department who specialize in American literature recommended that six American courses be added, Black American Writers and five upper division period and cultural surveys—Colonial and Federal, American Renaissance, Realism and Naturalism, Early Twentieth Century, and Contemporary. With the exception of Colonial and Federal, which is slightly less popular than the others, these courses have almost always enrolled to the departmental maximum of thirty students and sometimes over this. Students are attracted to these courses both by the instructors, some of the best and most popular in the department, and by their feeling that American literature is closer to their own interests than English literature. Our fall 1974 enrollment in one section each of Colonial and Federal, Realism and Naturalism, two sections of Contemporary, and one section of Black American Writers was approximately 140 students, about 18 percent of the total enrollment in all upper division courses. And these courses enrolled more nonmajors than majors.

Over the past three years, only a few courses have been added, most to meet the special interests and needs of students. Approaches to Literature was added primarily to prepare majors in practical criticism; it has been offered four times and its average enrollment is twenty-seven students per semester. Most of the students enrolled are English majors, who want to learn to read more closely and write better critical papers. The Bible as Literature was added for students from all departments who wanted to study the Bible. It has been popular, enrolling an average of twenty-five students, many of whom are nonmajors. Both Minority Voice in American Literature and African Literature are popular also, although neither has been offered very frequently so far. The course added during this period that enrolls the largest number of students is Fiction into Film, a variable credit course, offering two or three semester credits. The literature and films taught in the course vary, but the emphasis is on the translation of literature into film. This fall, the course, taught in the evening college, enrolled about seventy-five students, most of whom are nonmajors. Virginia Commonwealth has a large and well-known School of Fine Arts, and thirty-two of the students enrolled came from this school. The two instructors who teach this course both have good reputations among students, and film is a current interest of many of our students.

Most of the courses the department has added for the past four years, from 1970-71 on, have been particularly attractive to students: almost all seem to appeal to the current student interest in American literature (the more contemporary the better) or to the interests of a particular group of students, e.g., Black American Writers, Minority Voice, or Fiction into Film. Perhaps we should plan more of the curriculum around student interests, to broaden scope, without, insofar as possible, lowering quality.

We have also modified course requirements for both our B.A. English majors and B.S. in secondary education majors. Until fall 1972, B.A. majors were required to take thirty hours of upper division courses; within these thirty hours, they had to take Shakespeare; either Chaucer or Milton; and either Modern Grammar or History of the English Language. Since fall 1972, these specific course requirements have been dropped; B.A. majors must still take 30 hours of upper division courses, but now 24 of these must be distributed among the following four areas: English Literature; American Literature; Comparative Literature; and Linguistics, Criticism, and Advanced Writing. In essence, we have given the B.A. major more choice by eliminating specific course requirements, but by distributing credits more evenly have guaranteed more breadth in the major. In addition to their professional courses, secondary education majors must also take a minimum of six semester hours from each of the areas named above; they are, however, somewhat more restricted in that under the Linguistics, Advanced Writing, and Criticism block, they must take at least one linguistics and one advanced writing course (normally, Modern Grammar and Advanced Composition).

Because of these distribution requirements, our majors take a variety of courses. Some courses, however, are more popular with majors than others. A number of majors take figure courses, especially Chaucer and Shakespeare. Chaucer is taught by the first instructor in the department to win the ADE-MLA award for teaching lower division courses, a fact that accounts for its popularity. And on a recent departmental survey, a number of majors listed Shakespeare as the course that appealed to them most. Courses in the American literature sequence are also popular with majors, for the reasons previously discussed. The most popular courses in the comparative literature block are The Bible as Literature, Comparative Literature, and, quite often, foreign literature in translation. Our majors frequently take French and Russian literature in translation, probably welcoming the opportunity to study a foreign literature without having to achieve advanced proficiency in the language. In the Criticism, Linguistics, and Advanced Writing block, Modern Grammar is especially popular with majors, as is Approaches to Literature. Creative writing, especially short story and poetry writing, is growing in popularity, probably because both a coordinator of the creative writing program and a poet who has published a good deal were recently added to the staff.

A number of our upper division courses appeal especially to nonmajors. All the American literature courses, especially the modern and contemporary ones, are in this group. Black American Writers draws a number of nonmajors, probably because of the large number of Black students at Virginia Commonwealth and because it is cross-listed with Afro-American Studies. Both Modern Grammar and Introduction to General Linguistics are also fairly popular with nonmajors. This fall, these two courses drew two students from the School of the Arts, one from the School of Community Services, three from the Business Education program, and students from the School of Arts and Sciences majoring in biology, French, mass communications, mathematics, philosophy, psychology, and sociology. The most popular English course for nonmajors is Fiction into Film, for the reasons discussed above. As a department, we do not have particular courses designated for nonmajors, but these students are attracted to courses other than the standard English literature surveys; courses that appeal to a particular group of students, such as Black American Writers or Fiction into Film; courses that are modern or contemporary; and courses of technical interest, such as Modern Grammar or Introduction to General Linguistics.

Enrollment in all upper division courses has risen approximately 20 percent since 1970-71. This increase is probably attributable to the increase in the number of advanced courses offered each semester, from 21 in the fall of 1970 to 28 in the fall of 1974, and to the wider variety of these courses. Thus, the strength of the upper division curriculum is the variety it gives the students. One of its weaknesses has been that it was too exclusively course-centered; until the present, the only way a student could fulfill requirements was by taking classes that met two or three times per week. On 20 September 1974, the Departmental Curriculum Committee approved 24 courses—all the English and American literature surveys, the major authors courses, the three novel courses, three drama courses, and the three linguistics courses—for credit by proficiency examination. The Committee is also presently considering other nonclass options: one such option would be reading list courses, in which students attend no classes and study without faculty supervision the works on an assigned reading list. This option, along with credit by examination, might appeal particularly to students who are presently able to take only a few advanced courses per year in our evening college. Another option would be independent study courses, in which students would work on a literary or linguistic area under the supervision of a faculty member, submitting a report and/or taking a special examination.

The options discussed above notwithstanding, most of our students will continue to educate themselves largely through attending classes. Realizing this, the Curriculum Committee is considering a major revision of the present courses, as well as the addition of others, attempting to broaden a curriculum that presently overemphasizes literary history to the exclusion of other approaches. The period surveys might be revised to emphasize the relationship between literature and its philosophical and cultural contexts. Thus, American Literature, Contemporary, could become

American Thought in Literature: Existentialism and Ethnic Consciousness. A study of the impact of existentialism on post-World War ii literature and culture, and the development of an ethnic consciousness among American writers to the present.

Surveys in English literature might be similarly revised: courses such as The Medieval Universe: The Literature of Church and Castle; The Renaissance: The Literature of Plenitude; Romanticism: The Literature of Imagination; and The Victorian Frame of Mind: Response to Change would replace the present surveys of Medieval, Renaissance, Romantic, and Victorian literature. Courses emphasizing the relationship of literature to particular aspects of culture might also be added; for example, studies of the two-cultures' controversy, literature and law, and literature and music. The offerings in literary genres might be expanded to include courses in tragedy, comedy, satire, biography, short story in English, etc., and the writing program might include such courses as Writing Nonfictional Prose, Publishing Practices and Procedures, and Technical Writing. Linguistics courses, such as English Language for Teachers and Regional and Social Dialects in American English, might also be added, and courses in criticism would be expanded.

Our new curriculum is still in the planning stage and will probably change considerably before it is implemented. Some of the genre courses, for example, may never be added because there simply is not enough student interest in them; some of our faculty may object to revisions of the surveys, on the grounds that they are already teaching all they should about the relationship between literature and culture; and we may find that the suggested linguistics courses would be better placed in our new graduate program.

As we have realized in the last few years, changing a curriculum is a slow process, especially after a fairly conventional set of courses has been established. But we have changed a good deal in the past five years, and may have to change a good deal more in order to keep student enrollment. As a department, we need to know more about determining accurately students' interests and needs and to learn more about how to adapt ourselves and cooperate with each other in order to fill these needs. The weakness in our curriculum is that we still do not know enough about how to adapt ourselves or, for that matter, what to adapt to; its strength is that we have learned and adapted as much as we have.

C. W. Griffin
Director, Freshman English

Typical Courses Added in the Last Five Years
English Literature I, II, III
Medieval Epic and Romance
Introduction to General Linguistics
Black American Writers
American Literature I-V
Approaches to Literature
Bible as Literature
Playwriting
Minority Voice in American Literature
African Literature
Fiction into Film
Topics in Literature
English Novel, Eighteenth Century
English Novel, Nineteenth Century
Junior Seminar

Typical Courses Dropped in the Last Five Years
Freshman English for Engineers
Review of English Fundamentals

Most Popular Courses
The American Renaissance
American Literature: Realism and Naturalism
Early Twentieth-Century American Literature

Contemporary American Literature
The Bible as Literature
Black American Writers
Chaucer
Creative Writing
Fiction into Film
Modern Drama
Modern Grammar
Shakespeare
Romantic Literature
Modern Poetry

Least Popular Courses
Renaissance and eighteenth-century survey courses

Courses Most Attractive to Nonmajors
Black American Writers
Creative Writing
Fiction into Film
Introduction to General Linguistics
Modern Novel
Shakespeare
Bible as Literature
American Literature

Major Changes in Curriculum
(1) Specific requirements for majors have been dropped; (2) the advising system has been changed to encourage the taking of electives which will prepare students for a career outside the teaching profession.

19

Virginia Polytechnic Institute and State University

The latest freshman class to enter numbers twice as many declared English majors as the previous entering class contained.

Chairman Wilson Snipes
Virginia Polytechnic Institute and State University
Blacksburg 24061

Full-Time Faculty 53

Calendar Quarter

Type of School Public research university

Requirements for Major 57-75 hours, including Types of Discourse and Literature, English Literature Survey, American Literature Survey, six hours from each of the following five areas: English Literature through the Renaissance, English Literature of the Seventeenth and Eighteenth Centuries, English Literature of the Nineteenth and Twentieth Centuries, American Literature, Language and Writing. No comprehensive examination.

English has been taught, of course, ever since the founding, in 1872, of what has come to be known as Virginia Polytechnic Institute and State University. The growing importance of this curriculum parallels the emergence of its parent institution as one of the two comprehensive universities in the state of Virginia. Few major universities have undergone such radical changes of image and program as those occurring on the Blacksburg campus. Once known chiefly for preeminence in agricultural and engineering studies, it now houses seven colleges, Arts and Sciences being much the largest. Once almost exclusively male, women are now one third of the enrolled students. Once requiring military training for all able-bodied men, its Corps of Cadets now includes only three percent of the total enrollment. Furthermore, these changes have taken place very recently, during the 1960's and 1970's, contributing to a surge in enrollment which has doubled the size of the university (to 17,000) during the past ten years. Because some of these changes have had a bearing on the history of English studies at Virginia Polytechnic Institute and State University, it seems appropriate to furnish these details as a brief background for a look at the English department itself.

The English department is—as a degree-granting department—very young. For 90 of the 102 years of Virginia Polytechnic Institute and State University history, English was a service department, generally boasting a capable and dedicated staff but offering very few English courses above the sophomore level. In 1962, however, the A.B. degree in English was authorized; and the twelve years since have seen a flourishing growth in the size and influence of the English department.

Beginning, twelve years ago, with a handful of English majors, the department has seen an increase to the number of 300. Where the first advising activities consisted largely of guidance from the department head and/or his secretary, a staff of fifteen English advisers now coordinates and assists the academic activities of its charges. Minimum quarter hours of required English study have risen from the original 45 to the present 57 hours, with the maximum set at 75 (of a total of 189 required for graduation).

The first two years of college English study are prescribed, the last two broadly elective. A full year of freshman English—entitled Types of Discourse and Literature—is designed to strengthen existing student skills in writing ability and reading appreciation. The sophomore year finds each English major studying the full range of English and American literature in two distinct, year-long survey courses. In these freshman and sophomore courses, the English major is usually outnumbered by students from other university departments, who are required to take the freshman English and who may elect—or be required by their departments—to take some part of the sophomore English offerings.

From this solid platform of general studies in English, the major launches into a more diversified program during his last two years. Entering the second half of his college career, he is expected to possess 27 quarter hours of English credit, nine in the freshman course and 18 in the two literature surveys. Henceforth he will acquire six hours (generally 2 courses) in each of five areas, as follows: Literature through the Renaissance, Seventeenth and Eighteenth Centuries, Nineteenth and Twentieth Centuries, American Literature, and Language and Writing.

The four-year curriculum is designed to proceed from the general to the particular, the basic to the specialized. After the required introductory courses (freshman and sophomore), the junior level literature offerings are frequently period courses, with genre courses and the study of individual authors reserved for the senior level. This system of classifying courses is, however, not rigid.

What is the strength and what is the weakness of such an overall plan? The answer to both is the same: its flexibility. On the debit side, a student conceivably could satisfy his Area I requirement without Shakespeare or Chaucer. In such cases (which are rare), the earlier survey courses prevent him from total lack of exposure to the major figures and movements of literature.

The strength of the program likewise stems from its flexibility. Its comparative freedom of choice at the upper level appeals to the present generation of students. This same freedom makes it possible for "co-op" students—those who alternate quarters of work and college study—to make English their curriculum. The general convenience to English majors in scheduling their classes and conforming with registration processes is also a factor not to be ignored.

To discuss this program as a gem involves the need to examine its setting— College Core Curriculum Requirements for English majors. English majors, like every other Arts and Sciences student, must undertake successfully a year of mathematics study, a year of science, and a year of foreign language (to which the English department adds a second year). They must also pass twenty-four hours of social sciences courses, half of which must be in the same department. Finally—though this is a departmental requirement rather than a college one—there is the need for a minor of twenty-seven hours preferably in arts and sciences or education, with occasional exceptions being made for architecture or business.

What is "saving" the English program at Virginia Polytechnic Institute and State University, in the face of widespread criticism of English study in colleges and universities? That *something* is saving it seems evident. Its numbers have resisted inroads by newly created, competitive programs—speech, theater arts, communications, etc.—without notable decrease. Even the formation of a College of Education drained away comparatively few of the English majors interested in a teaching career. For the past several years, the English enrollment has hovered at or near the 300 mark. Possibly significant and certainly interesting is the fact that the 1974 freshman class numbered twice as many declared English majors as the previous entering class contained.

Some reasons for the sturdiness of the program seem obvious, others speculative. Its resistance to attrition in numbers is partly due to the university's steady growth, especially in the proportion of women to men. The program itself is under constant reexamination in order to meet the needs of its students which fluctuate in response to personal and national pressures, notably from unemployment. Still further, traditional programs of study suffer less flak in a state such as Virginia which, basically conservative, cherishes traditional values and landmarks. In this connection, it is perhaps pertinent to note that eighty percent of our students come from Virginia. This may help account for the fact that among the most popular offerings of the English department are courses in the major British authors, notably Shakespeare and Milton. Interest in American literature is also strongly evident, both at the sophomore survey level and in such courses as Southern Literature and Major American Writers. On the other hand, Old and Middle English classes have much weaker appeal, as do many of the classes in eighteenth-century English literature.

There has been no great pressure from students, departmental staff, or university administration to make major changes in the English program. Nevertheless, it has not remained static, its supporters being quite aware that English (like humanities studies in general) has become an endangered species. The general tendency to admit disadvantaged students to college has been acknowledged locally by the creation, during 1974, of a new course offering called Basic Writing Skills, which can be undertaken by new students deficient in areas of vocabulary and composition. A great deal of preparation was made for this course, which is administered by members of the regular staff assisted by graduate teaching assistants. It is flexible enough to be credit or noncredit, according to the amount of work mastered; and it can be used either to prepare for or to supplement the student's activities in regular freshman English classes.

The career dilemma of the English major is becoming increasingly serious. The teaching of English is becoming less viable as the main career opportunity, and English majors must fit other strings to their bows. The teaching option has been a popular variation on the standard English program; however, it seems appropriate to find other options, such as one that might combine appropriate business courses with a degree in English. Explorations in this direction are beginning with the thought that an English degree can be an asset in career areas where breadth of view and skill in communication can make an important difference in job competition.

William Grant
Administrative Assistant

Courses Added in the Last Five Years
Anglo-Irish Literature
Folklore
Afro-American Literature
Independent Study
Special Study
Basic Writing Skills

Courses Dropped in the Last Five Years
Advanced Composition
Agricultural Journalism
Literature of the British Commonwealth

Most Popular Courses
Shakespeare
Milton
Romantic Literature
The English Novel
Southern Literature

Creative Writing
Contemporary American Literature

Least Popular Courses
Eighteenth-Century Literature
Victorian Literature
Afro-American Literature
Modern English Grammar
Classical Drama

Courses Most Attractive to Nonmajors
Shakespeare
Southern Literature
Folklore
The Short Story
Creative Writing
Contemporary American Literature
Modern British Poetry

Major Changes in Curriculum
(1) Language and writing have been stressed more heavily by becoming an area equal with four others in the program of the English major; (2) maximum hours in the major have been increased from 66 to 75.

20

Washington University

The current trend is for more and more full-time faculty to participate in freshman offerings.

Chairman William Madsen
Washington University
St. Louis, Missouri 63130

Full-Time Faculty 28

Calendar Semester

Type of School Private research university

Major Requirements Thirty hours beyond freshman courses, including six hours of Major Authors and three hours of Shakespeare. No comprehensive examination.

Changing the curriculum, runs the weary saw, is like trying to move a ceme-
tery. The changes in our curriculum during the past four to six years have been
considerable, and yet they have disturbed few cadavers and prompted little controversy. The smooth transition can probably be attributed to the fact that all the
change has turned on two realizations, both widely endorsed by the English faculty: (1) No entering student's writing is so good that it cannot be improved; and (2)
since the department works with a wide variety of students with a wide variety of
goals, concentration on the highly motivated, professionally oriented major is un-
necessarily restrictive and just plain wrongheaded.

The first realization seized many of us simultaneously, prompted, I should
guess, by the long lines of freshmen waiting to argue their way out of our
two-semester composition requirement. The administration backed our insistence
that composition classes must be small, but our budget provided staff for a mere
two thirds of the arriving freshmen. Economic and administrative necessity had
somehow assumed the aura of a principle: not every student needs this course.
And so, many were exempted, ostensibly on the basis of test scores and writing
samples but actually on a curve corresponding to the number of classrooms we
could afford to sustain in any given term. When the composition requirement
came under fire during the years when everything did (and we lost our language
requirement), a large degree of student dissatisfaction could be traced, not to the
virtues or lack of them displayed in the writing courses, but to the humbling in-
equity of fulfilling a requirement so many were able to bypass. As we examined
the very idea of the requirement, we had to admit that if the course was important,
it was important for all and that there was something absurd about offering such a
course and then spending long hours selecting our most promising students to
release them from this valuable experience. So we suggested that the college faculty
reduce its requirement for the B.A. from six units of freshman composition to
"proficiency in reading and writing the English language." It has been left to the
department of English to certify this proficiency and to advise the student on how
best to achieve it. This has come to mean that virtually every freshman begins with
one semester of English composition in the fall or spring. With the new students
divided evenly between two terms by the dean's office, we were not only freed of
administering exemptions, we had sufficient staff to provide the course for every
freshman. Now, after three years and the consequent departure of most who had
avoided the course, the very idea of exemption from the requirement seems to
have faded from student memory. Personality conflicts between instructor and
student emerge with the usual regularity, of course, and no one has yet found a
way to make a composition class an exciting experience for one and all. But the
main source of discontent appears to have vanished, and most students seem to
have accepted E Comp 100 as the "introduction to college reading and writing" we
want it to be and to treat it as a necessary tune-up for the rest of their courses.

The one-term requirement for all has brought the added dividend of freeing
staff for two innovations, both of which appear to be thriving. Freshmen taking
one term of E Comp (and often no work at all with the language departments) seek
electives. Many sign up for our new Freshman Seminars in Literature, courses
limited to fifteen students and focused on materials of wide and general literary
interest. The second innovation, as far as our curriculum is concerned, has been
the expansion of offerings in composition at all levels; the most notable is our
burgeoning tutorial program. A student may register for regular meetings with a
tutor and earn three units of credit, or he may drop by informally at any time
during the term to discuss some current project or his writing proficiency

generally. Students who pass but do poorly in the freshman composition course can be required to register with a tutor before the department will certify their writing competence; others may be urged but not compelled to do so. (At the end of the term, the instructor checks a form carrying these alternatives; the student gets a copy and so do his adviser and the college dean). Similarly, instructors in other departments of the university have been urged to implement this "contingency grading" for students whose work is hampered by their writing: the earned grade is withheld until the student presents evidence of the assigned number of sessions with the tutor. Such referrals have been increasing and seem to work well in engaging our colleagues in the behalf of literacy. Indeed, the program has grown at such a rate (from 23 enrolled in fall 1972 to 102 in spring 1974) that our "extra" staff is now fully absorbed. We have never advertised this offering and now would be afraid to. It is, of course, very expensive—five to six students is considered a full course in a tutor's schedule—but the college administration has vowed to support the program until cutbacks are applied generally. Since both the Tutorials and the Freshman Seminars draw on staff previously budgeted, we have had to make no new demands on the resources of the college.

Most (but not all) of the introductory composition and tutorial instruction is done by second-, third-, and fourth-year graduate students, but our English faculty has never fallen into either a composition vs. literature or a graduate vs. undergraduate split. The current trend is for more and more full-time faculty to participate in the freshman offerings; the instructors in all the new advanced composition courses have been drawn from the entire faculty. These courses are not essentially different from the freshman course, but they have filled to capacity each term with upperclassmen who have perhaps discovered the need for such practice, have been referred by an instructor, or simply feel that good writing helps toward admission and success at professional schools. These new courses have unexpectedly solved the problem of where to assign the transfer student who must fulfill the college writing requirement but who would be most uncomfortable returning to a freshman classroom.

The steadily increasing interest of the department in composition during the past few years is related to the second of the realizations I mentioned: the English department must function in relation to the whole university and not focus its best efforts solely on the major en route to graduate school or even the major as such. We felt our responsibility to the traditional, serious English major, but we recognized as well that not all majors are "serious" or interested in the subtleties of advanced study and not all our students are majors. We could not neglect the business major who wants to challenge himself with some interesting reading and writing between his classes in bookkeeping and market finance. We had to be careful not to forget, in short, the role of the department in the liberal education of *all* the students in the university. As we began our curriculum review some four or five years ago, we realized that no single type of course could serve all of these students, and yet they must all somehow be accommodated.

Like many schools, ours had long ago adopted a course numbering system of 100, 200, 300, and 400 to coincide with the typical student's progress through college and to indicate, presumably, an increasing level of difficulty and sophistication. By the late 1960's, it had become apparent that few students actually pursued their educations or acquired them in such an orderly, sequential fashion. And few of our faculty believed any longer that for our subject the concept of steps and accumulation made much sense. Prerequisites had been eroded almost totally, the college urged us to open our classrooms to the interested if "unprepared" nonmajor, and many of us began to notice that a large number of the best students in our so-called advanced courses might in any given term be majoring in history, fine arts, or engineering.

We still share the college's numbering system, but we have done our best to educate student and adviser alike to think of our number levels as indicating the *type* of course designated and the probable goals of its audience. The only literature courses at the 100 level are the Freshman Seminars mentioned above; these are restricted to freshmen and recommended for those who do *not* presently think of themselves as majors (some samples from this term's 10 seminars: Modern Poetry and Song; Great American Short Fiction; The Mystery; Confidence Men in Literature). "A student who makes an early decision to major in English," runs the departmental handout, "may wish to begin work at the 200 level in his freshman year."

The central courses at the 200 level have traditionally been a pair of two-term sequences, one in major British authors and the other a selection of great books in translation. As we dwelt on the diversity of our enrollments, we decided to emphasize the major authors sequence by making it a particular recommendation for the prospective major and by stressing even further its concern for close literary analysis. (It has now been designated a required sequence for the English major.) The great books courses, on the other hand, had already begun moving toward the more general appeal and wider audience we came to associate with the 300 level.

The nature of the 300 level course and our effort to distinguish it in method, scope, and clientele from the 400 level has been the center of our curriculum revision. Here is some committee prose addressed to the student and his adviser:

> Courses in the 300 series may be of interest to majors and nonmajors alike. They offer an experience of reading and discussion as part of a liberal education in the traditional sense. Readings for a 300 course may be chosen entirely on the basis of the instructor's interest or his response to students' interest in writers not frequently studied together (e.g., Hemingway and Shelley) or topics not ordinarily taken up in period courses (e.g., Urban Novels and Pastoral Poems).
>
> Courses numbered 400 treat historical periods of English or American literature, or literary genres, or elements of the English language. As such, these courses are particularly useful to majors who expect to do graduate work in English or teach in high school. But they may also be attractive to a student who wishes to study a subject more fully than would be possible in 300 courses.

We introduce some twenty new courses at the 300 level each semester and only the most popular are repeated. Offerings at the 400 level, however, are spare and constant; they probably resemble most closely what many mean by "curriculum" in the sense of courses scheduled with predictable regularity. The basic distinction is between courses committed to covering a fully defined amount of material—where the aim is mastery of that material—and courses focused instead on the experience those enrolled may enjoy in the presence of good reading and apt instruction. Both types of courses are open to virtually all the students in the university (although the individual instructor may impose prerequisites if he wishes), but our hope has been that our audience in any given class will have been self-selected and can be addressed in terms of the stated end of that type of course.

Some sidelights which may illuminate the distinction further: many departments must share a problem we face—how do we continue to engage the interest of a diverse group of undergraduates with what is essentially a graduate faculty? And how can a faculty trained for scholarship be helped to sustain its interest in undergraduate teaching? The professor's specialty is very much to the point in 400 level courses. These are taught by the same instructor who offers the subject in a more limited and scholarly way to our graduate students; many graduate students begin their programs in 400 level courses, where they should encounter undergraduates with a similarly serious interest in the content of the course. At the 300 level, however, where the emphasis is on reading with enjoyment and critical understanding rather than on breadth of coverage, what is most required is insight, experience, and a fully responsible enthusiasm—not expertise. In fact, many of us had noticed that it was often the very weight of our specialization that became insupportable in the undergraduate classroom, frequently as much for teacher as for student. It seemed that most faculty should be qualified to work with most literary materials at the 300 level, and so we have had a Miltonist teaching Yeats, an Americanist doing Chekhov, Brecht, and Genet, a specialist in Elizabethan drama drawing large classes on Faulkner, and a long line of scholars from earlier periods pursuing their enthusiasm for various modern poets. Virtually every member of the department has taught the 300-level Shakespeare course—all in what we hope has been the true amateur spirit, and all to the end of providing interested and interesting faculty and students.

Developments of the last few months represent adjustments to what has been for us a fairly wide-open curriculum. Our efforts to meet the general interests of the general undergraduate seem to be fruitful (if one may judge by a brief span of 3 or 4 years), and our attention has turned back toward our serious major and his future in graduate school and beyond. The Major Authors of English Literature course, with its bent toward practical criticism, is now required of all majors. And lest the absence of other prerequisites and distribution requirements lead the major toward self-indulgence, he is required to include a semester of Shakespeare in his program. But the voices of those who would emphasize the student's preparation for graduate school must compete with those who sense the pressure of the market and note the tendency of the student body to seek usable skills. Maybe we shouldn't be so hostile to journalism after all; maybe there is such a thing as Business English, Engineering English . . .; perhaps we have no right to ignore these legitimate student needs. And so this report can only be a communiqué from a vehicle very much in transit.

Richard Ruland
Professor

Courses Added in the Last Five Years
Composition Tutorial
Argumentation
Introduction to Journalism
Literature Seminars for Freshmen
Major American Writers

Courses Dropped in the Last Five Years
Courses with specific titles (e.g., Irony and Satire) were dropped and replaced by courses with more general titles (e.g., a series called Topics in English and American Literature).

Most Popular Courses
Modern Drama
The Bible as Literature
American Literature (except Colonial Period)
Shakespeare
Composition
Milton
Chaucer

Least Popular Courses
Colonial American Literature
Sixteenth-Century English Literature

Whitman College

Each member of the department has the highest degree of individuality with regard to the matter of what he teaches, how he teaches, and how he deals with his advisees in the development of their programs.

Chairman Walter Broman
Whitman College
Walla Walla, Washington 99362

Full-Time Faculty 7

Calendar Semester

Type of School Private liberal arts college

Requirements for Major 33-34 hours, including four courses in English literature, one course in American literature, two courses in Chaucer, Milton, and Shakespeare, one course in literary criticism or history of the English language, and three additional courses in English. Comprehensive examination required.

The requirements for a major in English consist of those traditional courses in literature such as the two-course survey of American literature, the four-course English literature survey, and the two-semester course in Shakespeare and those courses which are designed each year by the professor, with the approval of the department, and taught under the headings of Special Authors, Special Studies, and Senior Seminar. In the last year, the department has changed its requirements and the nature of its survey courses in an attempt to represent more justly this relationship between the courses taught every year and those dealing with special subjects which change from year to year. What follows is, first, the old requirements for the major and, second, those currently in effect:

> The major: Courses must include three period courses, one author-centered course, one types or special studies course, English 95, 96, and three additional courses, for a total of ten courses. Of these, there must be one course in each of the following areas: Renaissance, Restoration and Eighteenth-Century English, Nineteenth-Century English, and American. Also required are a reading knowledge of a foreign language on the college intermediate level and familiarity with a reading list of works selected by the department.
>
> The major study: Students are required to take the four courses constituting the sequence in English literature, English 45, 46, 47, and 48; one semester of the sequence in American literature, English 79 and 80; two semester courses of the four semester courses devoted to Chaucer, Milton, and Shakespeare, English 60, 61, 63, 64; one semester of literary criticism, English 95 and 96, or of the history of the English language, English 88; three additional courses in English, one of which may be a course numbered from 21 through 28. A course in literature offered by a department of foreign language may be substituted for one of the three elective courses. Also required is a reading knowledge of a foreign language on the college intermediate level, as indicated by the completion of the intermediate year of study or the successful completion of a test of reading proficiency.

Whatever a student gains from a study of literature is almost wholly a result of what the individual instructor sees as important in his particular material; that importance can be expressed in a study of Scandinavian drama, for example, as well as it can be expressed in a study of Shakespeare or Medieval and sixteenth-century literature. At the same time, there seems to us a value in the requirement that majors take a group of courses which serve as a kind of common experience or basis for further reading and discussion. Thus, the upper level courses, whether in Shakespeare, Milton, or Chaucer, or a Special Studies course in myth, while generally having no specific prerequisites, assume the student's sophisticated ability to read and discuss literature, a sophistication he may gain by taking these survey courses.

Actually, enrollment in these survey courses has remained high even during the years they were not required. The attitude of advisers has been that their students work from the broad foundation which these survey courses offer and so the student intending to major in English has generally taken these courses as a sophomore while also taking a Special Authors or Special Studies course in a subject which interests him and which he knows may well not be taught again while he is at Whitman. He might, for example, at the beginning of his major program, take Medieval and sixteenth-century literature as well as the upper level Special Authors course in Joyce; he is taking the first course to work toward a specific beginning requirement of the department, while taking the second because of his particular interest.

Because the department is made up of only seven members, the requirements for the major and the nature of the specific upper level studies are determined by the entire department. These special upper level courses reflect, as I suggested above, the particular interests of the instructors involved, but are also considered in terms of some balance in the material being offered that year. For example, we try not to offer in a single year several upper level courses in twentieth-century literature, and we have found, for the most part, that the two-semester course in Shakespeare makes seminars on that author impractical. Considerations are, however, made from year to year giving both students and faculty a certain voice in what will be offered. I feel certain that if student interest in a Shakespeare Seminar, for example, was genuinely evident, the department would carefully consider offering such a course. The design of the Seminar or Special Studies course is not dependent upon material from the field of literature. Thus, last year one of the Special Studies courses dealt with material from motion pictures, while the Senior Seminar dealt primarily with material from Jungian psychology. Each course reflected directly the interest of the instructor as well as the feeling of the members of the department that such courses could be profitable for both majors and nonmajors. The following are descriptions of those courses:

Development of the Art of the Cinema

One or more classic films will be shown each Monday night and discussed in class the following Tuesday and Thursday. Discussion will focus chiefly on the literary aspects of the films—i.e., dramatic structure, characterization, theme, symbolism. Film scripts, whenever available, will be assigned to supplement the screenings. A tentative list of the films and their directors: *The Birth of a Nation* (Griffith), *Potemkin* (Eisenstein), *Metropolis* (Lang), *Modern Times* (Chaplin), *The Blue Angel* (von Sternberg), *Grand Illusion* (Renoir), *Citizen Kane* (Welles), *The Seven Samurai* (Kurosawa), *Hiroshima, Mon Amour* (Resnais), *Jules and Jim* (Truffaut), *Wild Strawberries* (Bergman), *Blow Up* (Antonioni), *Paths of Glory* (Kubrick). Critical papers, a midterm, and a final exam.

Myth and Archetypes

Investigation of theories of archetypes and myth as they are manifested in and applicable to literature. The semester will be devoted to a study of selected pertinent material from C. G. Jung, including *Flying Saucers* and *Memories, Dreams, Reflections*, and from such other works as the following: Freud, *Totem and Taboo*; Campbell, *Hero with a Thousand Faces*; Frye, *Educated Imagination*. Primary works: Grimms, *German Folk Tales*; *Moby-Dick*; *Wind in the Willows*; selections from the Bible. Short critical papers will be required.

Finally, a student—major or nonmajor—may elect to do independent work so long as the proposed work is approved by a member of the department willing to undertake such work and by the department as a whole. Approval by the department is sought to assure the value of the project and its consistency with other such projects.

The program for each major is determined—within the specific requirements of the department—by the student and his adviser. This adviser is picked by the student from any of the full-time, permanent members of the department, and thus the student is able to choose that member with whom he feels most comfortable. He and his adviser then decide the sequence of the required courses and discuss the nature of the electives—including nonmajor electives. Because Whitman is a small school, with an all-college enrollment of about 1,100 students, the major has the opportunity to get to know something of the instructors and so to make a choice that can reflect his own interests.

Again, I would like to emphasize the degree of individuality accorded each member of the department with regard to the matter of what he teaches, how he teaches, and how he deals with his advisees in the development of their programs. The required courses as well as the concurrence of the department members regarding the courses taught serve only as a framework for the personal expression of the instructor. This personal expression seems to me of supreme importance, since it is something we can offer which large universities generally cannot. We have no graduate programs in the school and thus the advantages in attending a small undergraduate institution must necessarily be emphasized through the possibility for close and extended work between an instructor and student.

Like all departments of the college, the English department offers the opportunity for a student to graduate with honors in his major study. The standards for graduation with honors are determined by the entire college faculty (the student, e.g., must have an accumulated grade point of 3.3 and must submit a proposal for his honors thesis to a three-member committee of the college). The proposal is approved by the member of the department with whom the student chooses to work. The student and this faculty member work through the writing of the thesis, and its final approval is dependent upon its acceptance by that faculty member. Another member of the department (or of a related department where appropriate) is generally asked to read the thesis and discuss it with the student, but final judgment rests only with the student's project adviser.

The courses that make up the curriculum for the major are by no means limited to majors; indeed, in most classes almost an equal number of majors and nonmajors constitute the class enrollment. Of course, those upper level courses with broad appeal (courses, e.g., dealing with material written in the twentieth century) tend to larger enrollments than courses on Milton, Chaucer, Browning, or a seminar in Jacobean and Caroline Drama.

Thus far this discussion has been concerned with the survey and upper level courses, with those courses primarily designed for the major; however, the department devotes more than a third of its teaching time to courses that are open to freshmen and that deal with literature on an introductory level. These courses, only one of which can count toward the major, also represent the individual interests of the instructor so that the nature of the course sections may vary. The following are descriptions of the three sections of our lowest numbered course, which reflect this diversity:

Section A: An examination of themes, motives, and forms, through reading and discussion. First semester, the Greek experience: Homer, *Iliad*; Aeschylus, *Oresteian Trilogy*; Sophocles, *The Theban Plays*; Thucydides, *Peloponnesian War*; Plato, *Republic*; Aristotle, *Ethics*. Second semester, the epic vision: Virgil, *Aeneid*; Dante, *The Divine Comedy*; Milton, *Paradise Lost*; Carlyle, *The French Revolution*; Tolstoy, *War and Peace*. Required papers and an examination.

Section B: A study of materials concerned with man's view of himself in isolation from his fellow beings. The course will be centered on class discussion out of which will grow four short critical papers each semester. Written works considered during the year may include nonfictional writings of Mailer, Freud, Jung, Eiseley, and Tillich; dramas of Shakespeare, Marlowe, Pirandello, and Chekhov; selected modern poetry; fiction of Lawrence, Hawthorne, Hesse, Faulkner, and Mann; and selections from the Bible, Tolstoy, and Gandhi.

Section C: Lectures and some discussion, with required papers and tests, on the theme of problems involved in becoming mature. Works studied will include most of the following: First semester: Flora Thompson, *Lark Rise to Candleford*; D. H. Lawrence, *Sons and Lovers*; L. P. Hartley, *The Go-Between*; J. D. Salinger, *The Catcher in the Rye.* Second semester: Shakespeare, *Hamlet*; O'Casey, *Juno and the Paycock*; John Osborne, *Look Back in Anger*; poems by Black, Wordsworth, and A. E. Housman; *Beginning with Poems.*

Similarly, the sections of the course Expository Writing differ depending on the inclinations of the instructor: some instructors have chosen to have their students read five or six books during the semester and to meet only twice a week formally, while others meet their class four times a week and have little or no assigned reading. The courses in Introduction to Poetry, Introduction to Fiction, and Introduction to Drama, as well as the two-semester world literature course, Masterworks of Literature, have, as the very nature of their titles suggests, more defined reading. Yet, specific materials are still not required of each section; where one might deal with the dramas of Aeschylus, another deals with Sophocles; where students in one section are reading Radin's collection of *African Folktales* and John Barth's *Chimera*, another section is reading Virgil's *Aeneid*, another *Burnt Njal.*

Each of these introductory courses has as a requirement at least four short critical papers. Thus, as in the upper level courses, primary emphasis is placed on the development of the student's ability to express himself. Even in the lower level courses, these papers are read and commented on by the instructor himself. Only the expository writing course is an exception to this number of papers in that it, of course, asks much more writing of the student—generally at least one paper each week.

For the past several years the nature of the major examinations has reflected this concern with interpretation and self-expression. The examinations have been divided along historical lines with the student writing the first day for three hours on two of three periods in literary history and for three hours the next day on two of three other periods. Selection of the periods (such as Medieval and Sixteenth-Century Literature, Seventeenth-Century Literature, American Literature to 1900) has been random and the student has not known on the first day from which three periods he will be asked to choose. Increasingly, portions of almost every examination have dealt with interpretation and discussion of a passage written during the period. For example, students writing on nineteenth-century British literature have often been asked to discuss critically Keats's poem "To Autumn" or a selection from a Browning monologue.

In the past year changes have occurred in both the structure of certain courses at the introductory level and in the requirements for the major, but these changes do not seem to me to suggest any significant change in attitudes of the members of the department. The one real addition to our curriculum, a course in the history of the language, reflects a need which most members have long felt. The splitting of the old Fiction, Poetry, and Drama two-semester course into three semester courses does not reflect any innovation but a response to the amount of material previously covered in two semesters. Even the dropping of the major requirement of a reading list represents a rejection of a technique which, employed for half a dozen years, did not seem necessary in light of steady enrollments in the survey courses. I might add that those of us who proposed the reading list as a basis for the comprehensive examination were those who proposed that it be dropped, that it had not served a useful function and so was an unnecessary appendage easily superseded by requiring the survey courses already being taken by a majority of students. A further reason for the elimination of the reading list was to make the comprehensive examination less formidable.

A concluding word should be said about course enrollments and numbers of majors over the years. Naturally, freshman enrollment in lower division courses is almost entirely by interest, though students here are often quick to comment on the nature of an instructor—how demanding he is, for example—and such comments affect even fall enrollments for freshmen to some extent. The courses in expository writing are the most popular because students hope to find some immediate and what amounts to superficial answers to problems of self-expression. The course in world literature which is combined with a course in history is also popular because it seeks to cross lines of discipline—something we might consider doing more often in both the lower and upper division courses. (I suppose the courses in Cinema and Myth and Archetypes described above represent a movement in that direction as did a special course, also offered with the history department, in the American West.) Because the catalog gives full course descriptions each year—a technique implemented by the Academic Dean several years ago—the freshman student is able to pick his courses more specifically with regard to material before ever coming on campus; such a technique perhaps helps to minimize hearsay faculty evaluation by students. All courses open to freshmen and nonmajors generally are limited to an enrollment of 30; again, the exception is Expository Writing, which has a class limit of 15. In probably two thirds of the classes this limit of 30 is not met but enrollment in these courses has remained relatively constant over the years.

What can be said of these enrollments is also true of our number of majors; what has affected course enrollments—interest in such disciplines as sociology and psychology—has similarly affected the number of our majors. The days of a class enrollment of 40 or more seem, except in unusual cases, to be gone; and no longer do we graduate 30 or 35 majors. On the other hand, enrollments and number of majors have risen somewhat just in the last two or three years. The number of declared majors (sophomore-senior) in April 1973 was, according to the registrar's office, 62; in April 1974, 71; this fall's number of declared majors is 51. (The Assistant Registrar explained that this fall's total is lower, of course, as the spring 1974 seniors have graduated, and sophomores who will declare a major in spring 1975 are naturally not reflected in the fall number.)

Whatever integrity characterizes my department is clearly evidence of the attitudes of the individual members; a department of seven is simply too small to hide the inadequacies of its faculty. This is not to say that such inadequacies have not or do not exist, but it is much harder for them to go unnoticed by majors, nonmajors, and members of the department. The problems which arise from a small English faculty in which each individual is given great freedom are not always small but they are unquestionably compensated for, over and over, by what the department can achieve for its students and its own members.

Michael McClintick
Associate Professor of English

Courses Added in the Last Five Years
History of the English Language
Other courses reorganized

Courses Dropped in the Last Five Years
The American West

Most Popular Courses
Introduction to Fiction
Shakespeare
Twentieth-Century Literature

Least Popular Courses
Specialized courses: Browning Seminar,
    Melville Seminar, Jacobean and
    Caroline Drama

Courses Most Attractive to Nonmajors
Shakespeare
Twentieth-Century Literature
Special Authors: Joyce, Faulkner, Mailer
Special Topics: Myth and Archetypes

22

Yale College, Yale University

Despite the difficulties, financial and otherwise, that are affecting American higher education, it seems that the study of English language and literature is alive and well at Yale College.

Chairman A. Dwight Culler
Yale University
New Haven, Connecticut 06520

Full-Time Faculty 65

Calendar Semester

Type of School Private research university

Requirements for Major Twelve terms of English courses, including no fewer than four from courses in English in major figures and periods up to 1800 and two from courses concerned with problems on one of the major literary forms or modes or dealing with literature in terms of language, the theory of criticism, or another unifying approach or idea. Method of final evaluation varies.

Yale College's English department has been engaging during the past few years in a reinterpretation and reorganization of two important programs. The more visible of these, in the course catalog at least, is the program for the standard major. Less obvious to the catalog browser but of equal or greater impact on the undergraduates we teach is the change in our basic freshman course. Both areas of change reflect trends in American education generally: the movement in the late sixties toward greater self-determination for students; and the countermovement now toward the partial reinstitution of more clearly defined structures.

In our requirements for the standard major we have, throughout this period of change, insisted on the necessity of historical knowledge, on the need for our students to extend their explorations in literature's "museum without walls." Too great a concentration on what is current is no less narrow than an exclusive concern with some limited period of the past. We have therefore always asked that English majors include in their programs four term courses in literature *before* a given date. In 1967-68, this date was (about) 1700; from 1969 until this year it was 1900; we have now moved it back to 1800. These are not magic numbers; but they do reflect the greater or lesser degree to which a general requirement helps to shape the individual program.

In 1970, as part of an emphasis on the solitary student, we abandoned the comprehensive examination, and made, instead, a one-term individual project mandatory for seniors. The project might involve enrollment in a special seminar; more frequently it was a matter of writing an extended paper (or poetry or fiction) or of carrying out a course of reading under faculty supervision. Here, again, we have found that (like other seekers of greener pastures) we were better off before. Not every student is able or, perhaps, should be able to devise and carry out a substantial piece of independent work in the field. Nor has it proved easy for advisers and students to match up satisfactorily in every case. With an increased number of students both within and outside the major and with a spate of demands in the early seventies for individual "courses" ad libitum, we found that the business of conducting tutorials, which should be one of the most interesting parts of a college teacher's job, became in fact a burden. There is very little to be said, educationally, for multiplying tutorials to the point where tutors (who usually have a full teaching schedule otherwise) cannot provide fully attentive guidance.

Our partial retreat, therefore, is a recognition of some hard pedagogic realities—centrally, that most students get along better with a more structured program than either they, or we, a few years ago, might have hoped for. We have retained the senior project as a strong option, open to students of proven ability; within that option we have provided not only tutorials, but a number of "senior seminars." Where, previously, the seminar has sometimes been a last resort for less ambitious seniors, we are now offering what we hope will be a set of exciting opportunities for well-qualified students. The senior seminars proceed on a near graduate level, assuming some background in the particular subject (this year, The Emergence of Romanticism, Nineteenth-Century Literature and Thought, Allegory, Problems in Fiction, The Post-Romantic Artist-Hero). The starting point of these courses is advanced, but they retain the more appreciative and less technical orientation that we believe is suitable for undergraduate students.

Although our faculty-student ratio has decreased slightly since 1969, this has not entailed a decrease in the number of courses we offer. In fact, we now offer 26 terms of lecture courses as opposed to 20 in 1969; 54 terms in seminars of limited enrollment as against 48; and ten, compared to six, courses in writing. We still give historical coverage first priority in our range of course offerings, but we are likely, today, to approach literary history in terms of continuities (themes, forms, modes) and individual authors rather than in terms of historical periods. The range and variety of topics means, we believe, that our requirements of four terms before 1800 and two in "forms and modes" ought not to be simply a matter of the student's checking off a few ineluctable requisites. We rely heavily on our system of individual advising to help each of our majors construct a program reflecting his own inclinations as well as a degree of historical and critical sophistication. Advising is centered upon the Director and the Assistant Director of Undergraduate Studies and a cadre of Departmental Representatives, one for each of Yale's twelve residential colleges. This means that, to a large extent, every English major can consult with someone who both knows the ropes and has time for him.

If a student's interests carry him beyond what the English department itself provides, he can incorporate into his major program courses in foreign literatures, related disciplines, and, often, seminars in a variety of special topics given under the auspices of the residential colleges. Our undergraduates are very rarely permitted to take graduate courses in English, and there are no courses cross-listed with those given in the graduate school. It is possible, however, for the student interested in secondary school teaching to meet certification requirements through the Teacher Preparation Program. Students whose interests crosscut the traditional categories of academia have available several major programs that often include English courses, for instance, the majors in Literature, British Studies, American Studies, and in History, the Arts and Letters. Interdepartmental and interdivisional majors are also possible on an individual basis. Those who desire greater concentration and a substantial amount of time (2 terms) for a senior project may, if they are qualified, choose the intensive rather than the standard major in English.

A university's English department is, of course, not exclusively an area of specialization; it is a resource and a set of opportunities for all undergraduates. Although no general rule requires nonmajors to take any English course whatever, we do, in fact, teach some ninety percent of all Yale College students. At the upper level, anyone who has completed an introductory English course (and with permission, some who have not) may take any of our lecture courses. Nonmajors may also enroll in the upper level seminars, whenever we have room for them. By far our broadest encounter with Yale College students, though, is in the freshman courses. A freshman with advanced placement in English who plans some other major is likely to choose the world literature course, English 29; some 380 students have done so this fall. The number is similar for English 25 (Major English Poets). This is the only course we specifically require of majors, but many other students take it out of general interest.

The largest single group of students with whom we deal is the population of the basic freshman course, English 15. That population is a varied and interesting one, and a continual challenge to the department. In 1969 this course was labeled "Literary Analysis and Interpretation," and was taught in small sections of fifteen students, all following the same prescribed syllabus. English 15, like the other freshman offerings, was taught and coordinated by full-time junior faculty members, with a few acting instructors (usually advanced graduate students) and lecturers to make up the needed quota of sections. In the atmosphere of revaluation and change of 1969 and 1970, this staff struggled to think out and re-design the basic course, to put it in better tune with students' secondary school preparation and with their interests; to make it less alien—a harsh word, but the right one—to instructors whose most recent training has usually been directed toward writing their own dissertations, rather than toward teaching freshman composition. The questioning and inventing of this group came to involve department members at all levels, and resulted in a new structure for the course, a revitalized affirmation of its aims, and a small but significant change in the staffing of all the introductory courses. First, English 15 jettisoned its traditional uniform reading list and was reconstituted as a collection of "freshman seminars." During the first two weeks of classes, all sections use the same text, so that the many students whose schedules are still unsettled may shift sections of English without serious inconvenience. After that, each section has its own syllabus, worked out by a particular instructor. This move seems to have solved two problems at once: there is (or can be) far less duplication for the student of course reading that he did in his later years of secondary school and the instructor can make the course material congenial to his own strengths as a teacher at the same time that he tries to meet the changing needs and interests of today's students. Since a number of the instructors are likely to be new to college teaching, this can help to turn bafflement into focused challenge.

Too often, freshman English seems to be what one teaches until one has enough seniority to escape; our change in staffing procedure may be of interest here. In 1969-70, no senior faculty taught freshman courses; in 1974-75, some ten are doing so. This is entirely voluntary on a professor's part; but those who have undertaken a term or two of a freshman course in the past few years have found it rewarding, and their presence on these staffs is a moral support as well as a source of useful advice for the newer members. It also helps us to cope with a Yale enrollment that has increased from 1,050 matriculants in 1969 to 1,320 in 1974. Since a few numbers do sometimes say volumes, I would call attention to the importance of changes in freshman English simply in terms of population. Last year, for instance, we had about 320 junior and senior English majors; but 480 students were enrolled in English 15. Most of these students will not major in English; the course is therefore a very significant portion of the department's outer face.

Another portion of that outward face that is perennially being revised is the course offerings in writing. In 1969-70, there was only one such course, the popular and successful "Daily Themes," and it was primarily restricted to seniors. It ran for a semester, and could be followed by one of five more advanced sections in writing poetry, fiction, or drama. The course now listed as English 80 is the daily themes course; but a glance at the succeeding catalog entries will show that while we have at the moment no playwriting course (one is offered by the drama department), we offer more in the way of writing instruction, including two seminars in the writing of nonfiction. In this way we are responding to current students' interests in journalism; we hope to enlarge our response as our resources permit. Still other writing courses are available among the residential college seminars (see "Typical Courses Added"). There is, however, no writing major at Yale, and only a limited number of writing courses can be included among the twelve terms required for the English major. One corollary of this restriction is that our writing courses are attended—as indeed they are designed to be—by students from a wide variety of fields.

Despite the difficulties, financial and otherwise, that are affecting American higher education, it seems that the study of English language and literature is alive and well at Yale College. We have been able in the last few years to increase the range of our course offerings (though we would like to offer more in the drama), to attract a growing number of majors, and to extend the opportunities we offer to nonmajors. Simultaneously (and continuously) we are actively readjusting our regulative structure so as to keep faith with the traditions of education at the same time as we adapt to the ever-changing society of which we are a part.

Paula Johnson
Assistant Director of Undergraduate Studies

Typical Courses Added in the Last Five Years
From Medieval to Renaissance
Tendencies in Modern Literature
Nonfiction Workshop
Literature and Psychology
The Post-Romantic Artist-Hero
American Humor
Androgyny in Literature*
American Writing in the Seventies*
Themes and Problems in the Mystery Tale*
American Literature and the Politics of
   Culture*
Readings in C. S. Lewis*
Journalism: The Art of the Fact*
The Craft of the Writer*
The Disciplines and Techniques of Nonfiction
   Research and Writing*

Courses Dropped in the Last Five Years
Theory and Practice of Fiction
Aspects of Fiction

*Available in Residential College Seminars.

Contemporary Poetic Theory and Practice
The American Renaissance
Autobiography and Testament
The Literary Use of the Bible
Playwriting

Most Popular Courses
Shakespeare
Writing courses
Romanticism
American literature
Modern literature

Least Popular Courses
Courses in authors and periods before 1700

Courses Most Attractive to Nonmajors
Freshman courses
Shakespeare
Modern literature

23

Yale University, Literature Major*

Literature X was genuinely different from any other course offered in literature at Yale.

Chairman Peter Brooks
254 York Street
Yale University
New Haven, Connecticut 06520

Full-Time Faculty 19**

Calendar Semester

Type of School Private research university

Requirements for Major Two terms from Area I, Man and His Fictions and Introduction to Theory of Literature; two terms from Area II, literature in a classical or modern foreign language; five terms from Area III, history and development of Western literature; one term from Area IV, non-Western literature; one term from Area V, literature and other disciplines; one or two terms of Area VI, the senior colloquium; one term from Literature 80 courses, Literature and Psychoanalysis; one additional term from Areas I-V or one term of a course in creative writing.

---

*A special interdepartmental major administered by several literature departments.
**The major has no full-time faculty members of its own, only parts of faculty from other departments.

The literature major at Yale is an interdepartmental program administered by a governing board with representatives from the several literature departments. It was begun by a group of teachers of different literatures who were dissatisfied with the almost exclusively national definition of literary study in the curriculum and who were critical of traditional great books or humanities courses, which in their assumptions about a great tradition extending from Homer to Beckett seemed to make of literature something inert and fixed for all time. Those who collaborated in establishing the literature major were interested in a program that would turn into interrogations what were usually accepted as givens, that would make the study of literature problematical and would address the question of its place among other human activities and functions. They wished to attenuate the isolation of much literary criticism, its self-containment, through a new engagement of literature's place in the encounter of consciousness and the world. The courses of the major seek, in various indirect ways, to pose the question, "What is literature?" and to elicit critical awareness about the ways in which it can be studied.

These concerns in particular inform the two introductory courses, Literature X, "Man and His Fictions," and Literature Y, "Introduction to Theory of Literature," which are ordinarily taken during the sophomore year. Literature X places the study of literature in the broad context of human fictions and fictionmaking, a range of activity and artifacts, including dreaming, games, role-playing, advertising, model-building, as well as literature. The word "fictions" is useful because its etymology (*fingere*) points to the two senses of our phrase "the made-up": the fabricated and the feigned. The course addresses itself to the project of human fictions, the need for "writing the world," and the relation of fiction-making to other forms of thinking, and to lying. The course uses a wide variety of literary texts, and some sub- and nonliterary texts: detective stories, science fiction, case studies by Freud, advertising slogans and icons. It makes use of juxtapositions—for instance, Sophocles' *Oedipus* and a Sherlock Holmes tale—in order to make analysis and evaluation more troubling and dialectical, to suggest structural similarities in different categories of fictions, and to make the student rethink criteria of value. It addresses problems of plot, the relationship of consciousness to things, the nature of textual "characters," the role of man as a sign- and sense-maker. The course is currently taught by five faculty from five different literature departments, each of whom leads a discussion group, and who take turns lecturing, once a week, to all the groups combined.

Literature Y, which follows Literature X, is a course in literary theory; it offers an ambitious and rigorous conspectus of the most important modern positions. It covers such topics as: literature, oral tradition, and the media; the theory of meaning and interpretation (hermeneutics); questions of genre, the mixture of forms and fusions of various arts; the structure and range of literary value judgments, and a critical analysis of Marxist, psychoanalytic, formalist, and structuralist approaches to literature. It is primarily a lecture course, supplemented by some discussion group meetings, and also uses the participation of guest lecturers to present certain critical positions.

Following these required introductory courses, a student essentially makes up his own program according to guidelines which are intended to help him establish some coherence in his course selections. He must build a foundation in the major texts, genres, and periods of Western literature, must gain some experience of a non-Western literature, and take at least one course in another discipline that might usefully be related to literary study. He must also pursue the study of at least one foreign literature at an advanced level, in the original language. The student, then, chooses courses from the various departments, keeping in mind the guidelines and consulting with the Director of Undergraduate Studies, shaping his program so as to educate himself in the main historical, theoretical, and methodological questions raised by his literary studies. In addition, the literature major itself provides a series of junior seminars, one of which must be taken by each major during his junior year. These have included such topics as Literature and Psychoanalysis; Realism and the Novel; Sociology and Literature; Defenses of Poetry in Renaissance Literary Theory; The Ancient Epic; The Discovery of a New Man in the Hispanic Literature of the Golden Age; Latin American Narrative in the Literature of Experiment. It is probable that the major will also require an additional seminar to be taken by all students in the first term of the junior year, a course in Texts and Interpretation which will move from practical questions in the reading and analysis of texts to larger questions of interpretation and the role of the interpreter. The course will use texts in several major languages; students will be responsible for those texts written in the language they know, but will also listen to presentations, aided by translations, on texts and languages they do not know. The creation of this course comes in response to a need stated by students themselves, who feel they need more training in analytical and rhetorical skills.

In the senior year, in addition to continuing their work in courses drawn from the various departments, students are required to take, in the fall term, a senior colloquium. This is designed to bring them together in a critical reflection on their work in the major and to develop a theoretical understanding of certain key issues in the study of literature. The colloquium is each year centered on one major problem in the understanding and interpretation of literature. The topic for 1973-74 was "Fictions of Confession"; that for 1974-75 is "Metaphor." The colloquium is taught by four teachers, each of whom directs a section of about 12 to 14 students, with occasional plenary sessions for presentations of a new unit of work. In the spring term of the senior year, the student normally writes a senior essay, an independent project carried on under the direction of a faculty member, which may grow out of the work he has done in the fall term colloquium. Those students who do not present a valid project for the senior paper have the option either of taking a further semester of work in the junior seminar area, or of pursuing further the study of a foreign literature at an advanced level.

An option within the Literature Major permits a student particularly competent in one or two foreign languages to pursue the comparative study of two national literatures. The introductory requirements and the requirement for the senior colloquium remain the same, but the emphasis in choice of courses from other departments is shifted slightly. One course in creative writing may also be counted toward the major.

As it now stands, the literature major is a structure that provides a beginning, some middle, and an end of a program and that provides some principles for the student's own structuration of the rest of the program. As such, it draws on the strength of the various Yale literature departments, encourages a wide acquaintanceship with the different modes of human fictionmaking, and places them in a perspective that suggests the need for critical theory and methodological self-awareness. In some sense, the courses belonging to the major exist in dialectical relationship to the courses drawn from the various departments: they attempt to problematize the study of literature, to ask questions that are usually assumed rather than openly addressed in more traditional departmental offerings, and to lead students to a high degree of self-consciousness about literary study.

An evident danger of such a program is the dispersion of the student's course of study that it may foster. The wide variety of courses taken by our students, in a large number of different departments, has been a source of vitality in that the students tend to bring to the courses sponsored by the major—and especially the Senior Colloquium—a range of interest, knowledge, and expertise. But it may be necessary in the future to have at the core of the curriculum further courses sponsored by the major itself in which all the students would participate. Already, the new required semester in the junior year on Texts and Interpretation moves in this direction. The point would seem to be to construct a backbone firm enough to provide coherence and logic while allowing the student maximum freedom in his choice of other courses.

The major began its formal existence in the fall of 1972, graduated its first group of seniors in the spring of 1974. It currently enrolls about seventy-five majors. The initial strength of the program was in the two introductory courses, Literature X and Literature Y. Literature X was genuinely different from any other course offered in literature at Yale, by its speculative engagement of the question of man's need and use for fictions, in its attention to "paraliterary" forms, in the breadth of its range and of its teachers' interests. Literature Y was the first course to offer a serious anatomy of the major modern schools of criticism and interpretation; it has indeed become a popular course for graduate students as well as undergraduates, since nothing really comparable yet exists among graduate seminars. These two courses have been taken by a variety of Yale undergraduates majoring or intending to major in very different fields. A vital experience in these courses has undoubtedly led many students to consider majoring in literature. The students who do major in our program tend so far to represent a range of abilities; the best of them are among the very best students at Yale. It is not clear what such students would have majored in before the existence of the literature major; in most cases, probably English or one of the foreign literature departments. It is no secret that enrollment in foreign literature majors has been in a nationwide decline for some years. The literature program may draw some majors away from the foreign literature departments, but it should also have the effect of steering more students into foreign literature courses since its guidelines include a rigorous language requirement. It is felt in the major that the inevitable necessity to read many works in translation must to some extent be compensated by the students' training in dealing with texts in at least one foreign language. The teachers of the major's courses come from many different foreign language departments as well as English and most often know the original of the text that they may be teaching in translation.

At its most successful, the literature major draws its vitality from its willingness to engage students with the kind of material and the subjects that most interest them and from its insistence that appreciation and commentary must lead to interpretive rigor and theoretical formulation. And at its best the major inculcates in its students a higher degree of awareness about why they read literature and what it means to talk about it critically than is usually the case. The major has been possible at all only because of the accumulation of strengths represented by the various Yale literature departments, and it has profited from the very great enthusiasm generated by the prospect and practice of faculty members from different departments working together in planning courses and programs and in teaching.

Peter Brooks
Director, The Literature Major
Associate Professor, French and Comparative Literature